Vintage Photos of Halloween, Volume 3

Wyatt Douglas

NOTE:

Many of these photos are nearly a hundred years old. In many cases the copies we came across were not in good condition. We've restored and color corrected them to the highest quality we could.

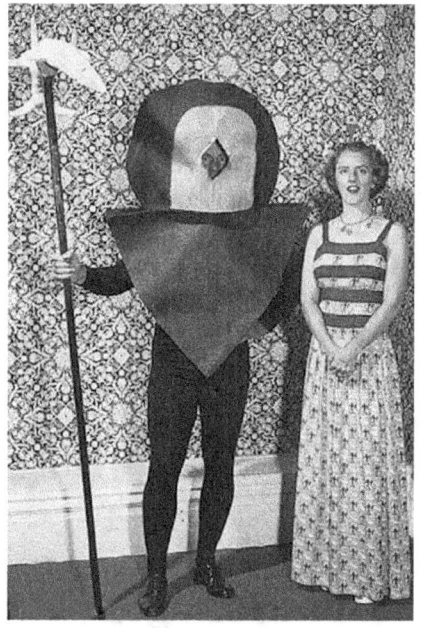

Copyright © 2018 Wyatt Douglas

All rights reserved.

ISBN: 1729732518
ISBN-13: 978-1729732519

Vintage Halloween Photos

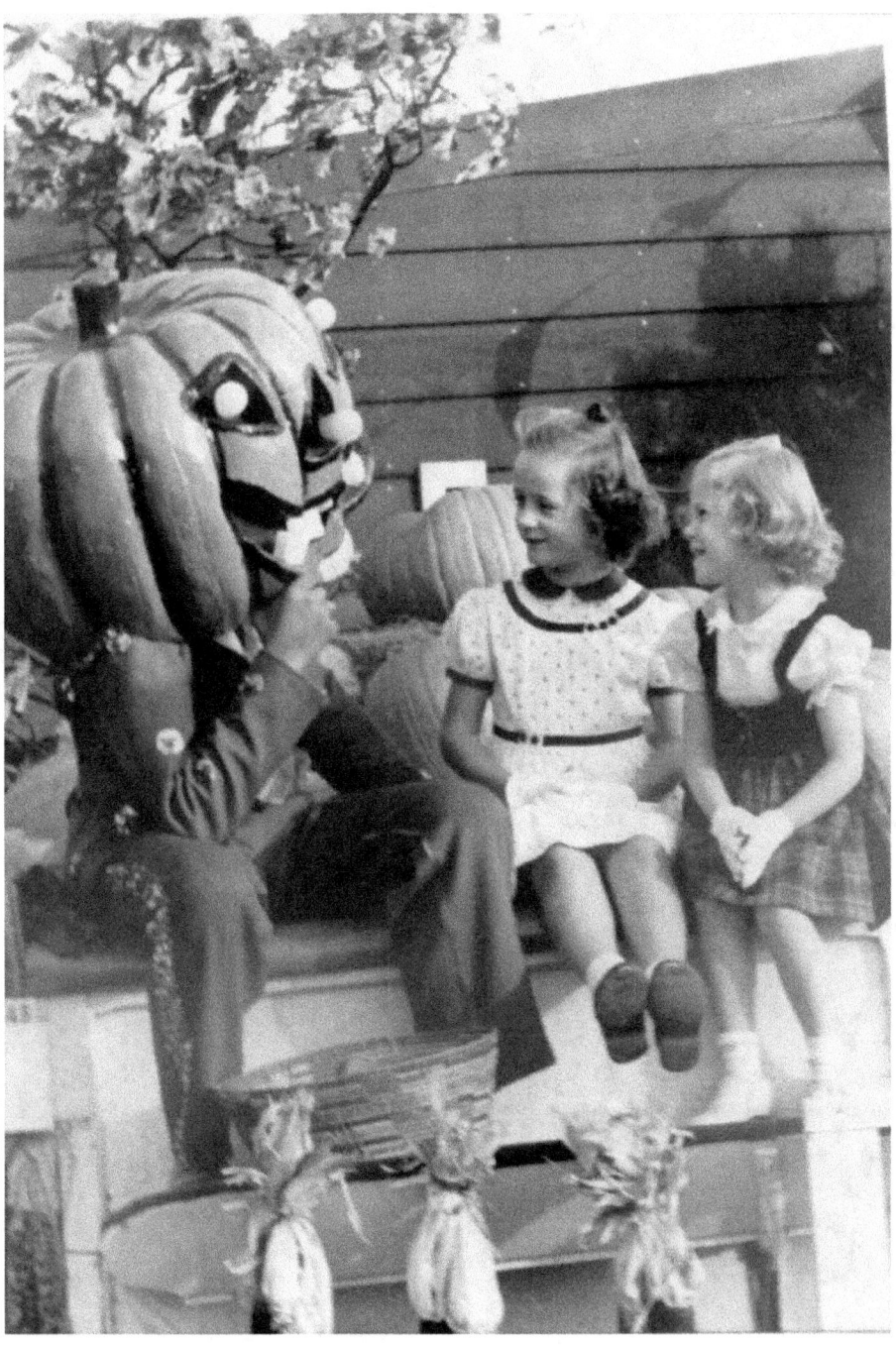

WYATT DOUGLAS

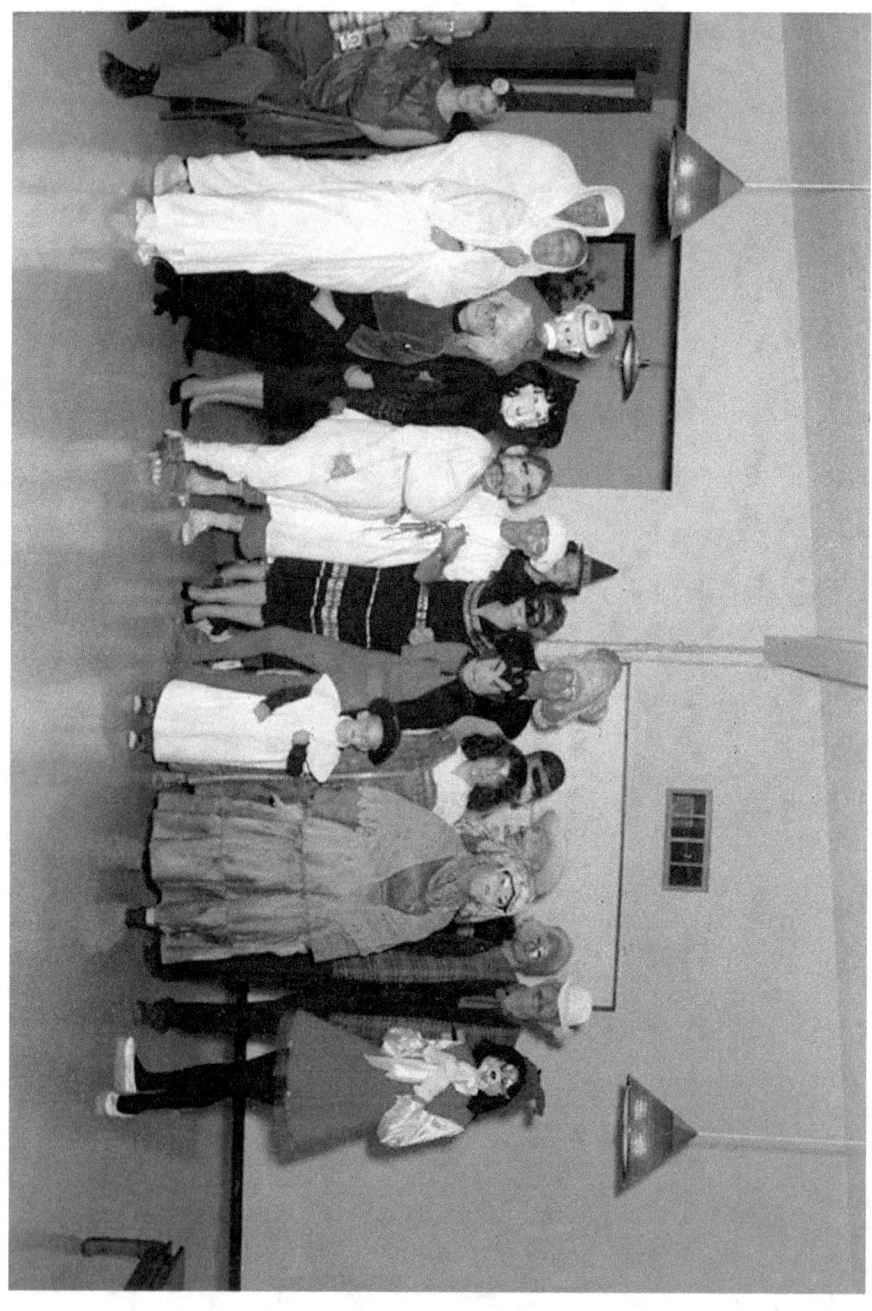

Vintage Halloween Photos

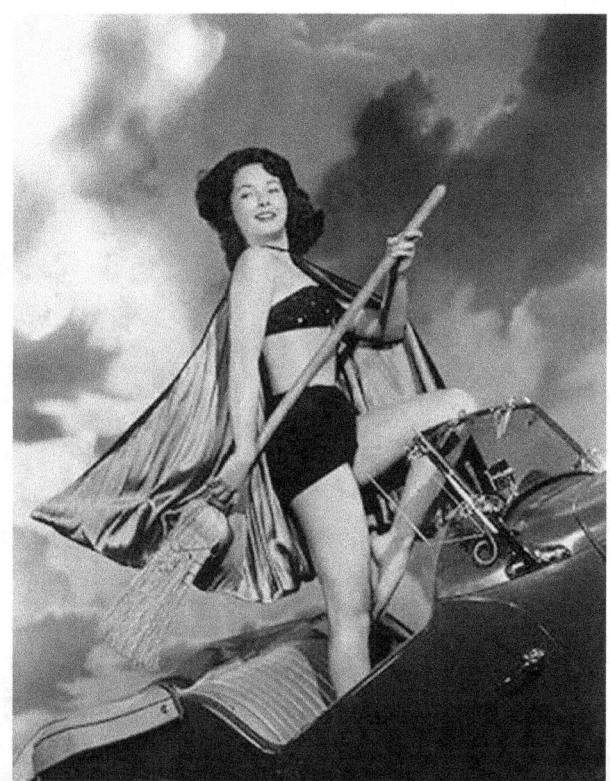

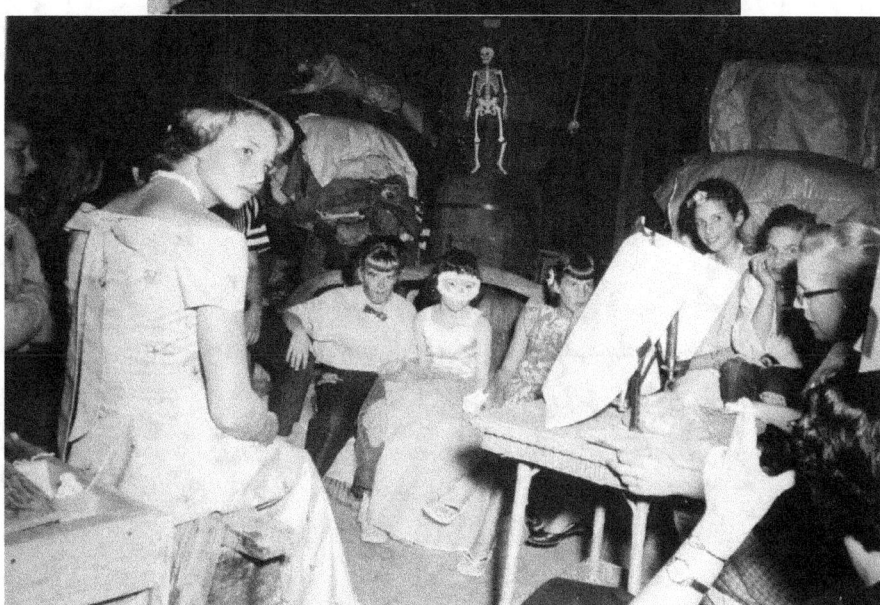

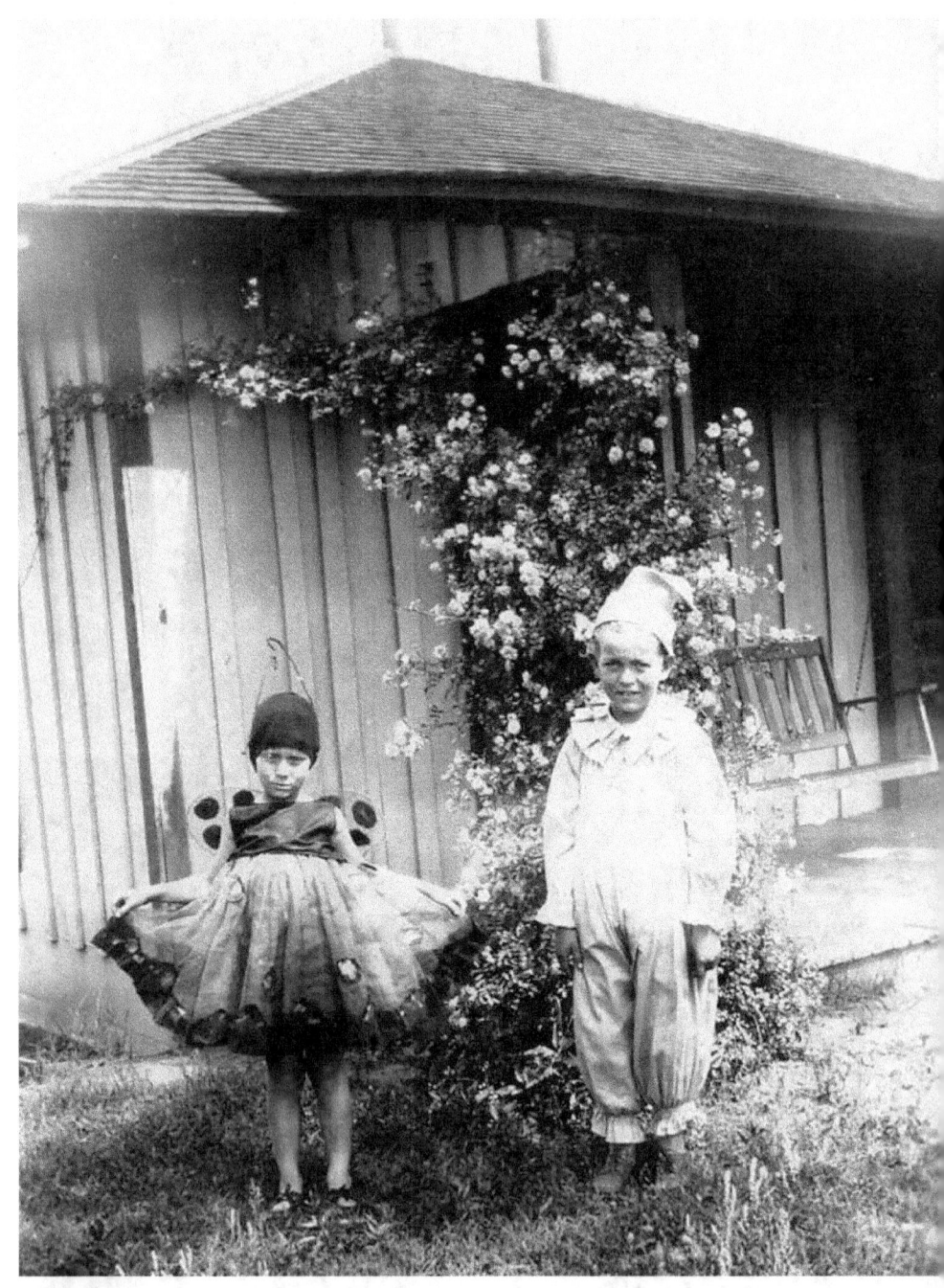

Vintage Halloween Photos

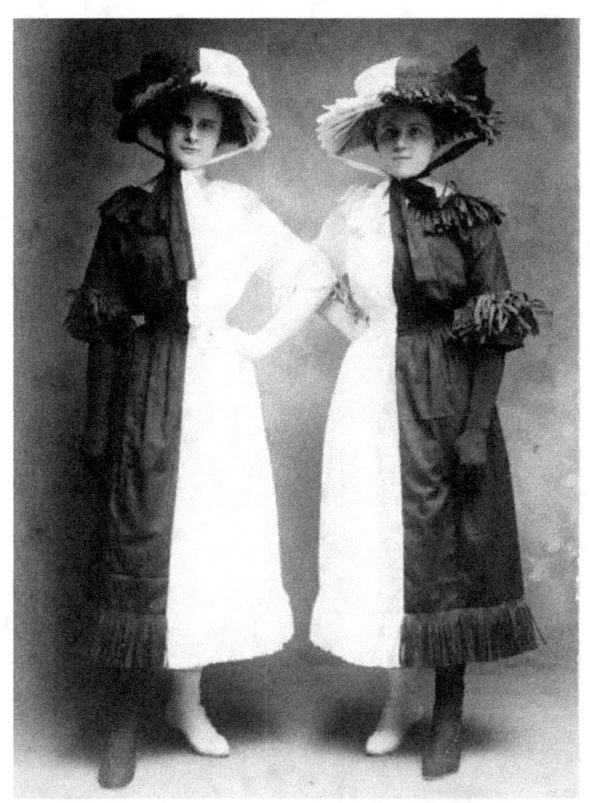

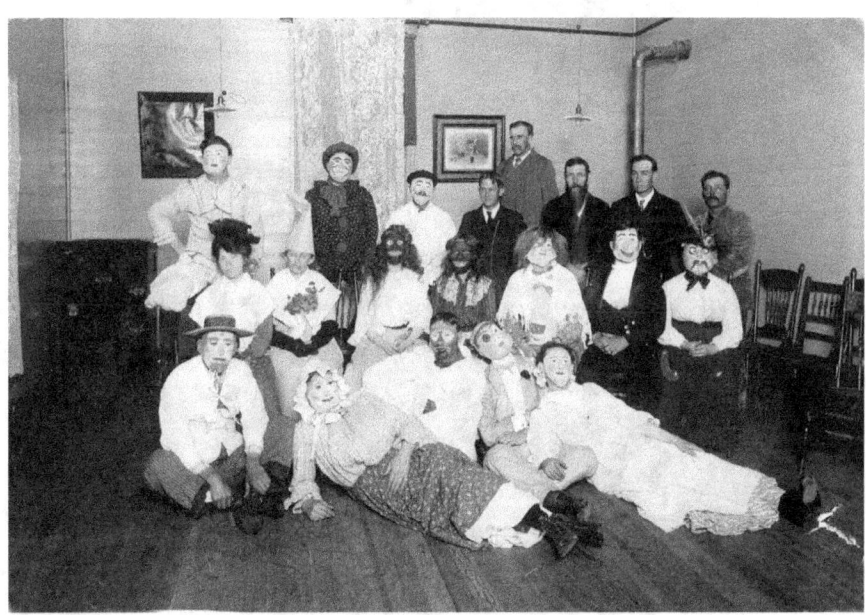

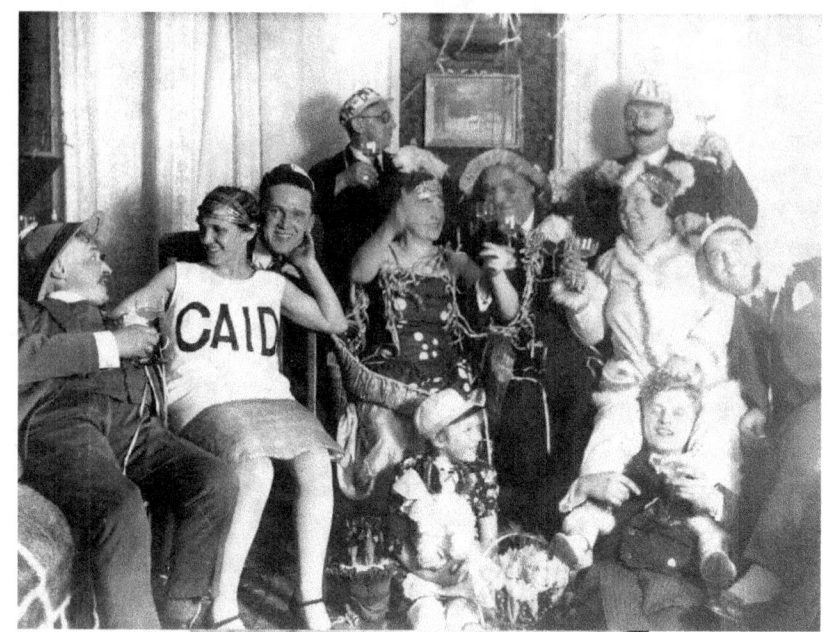

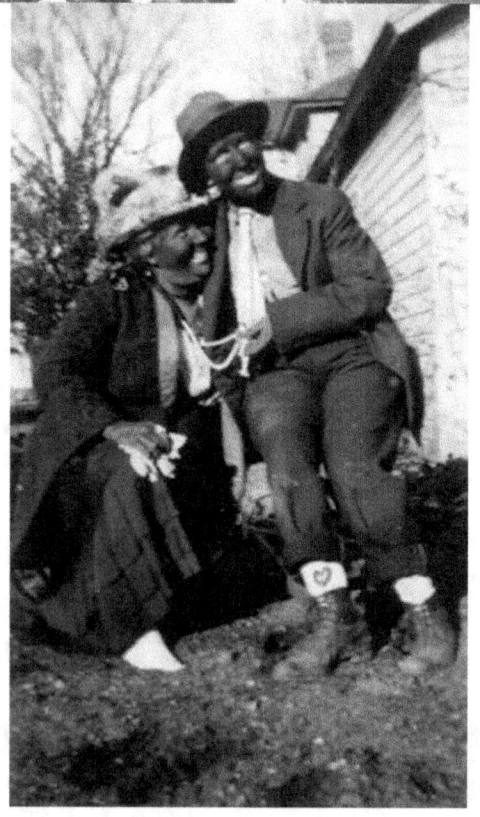

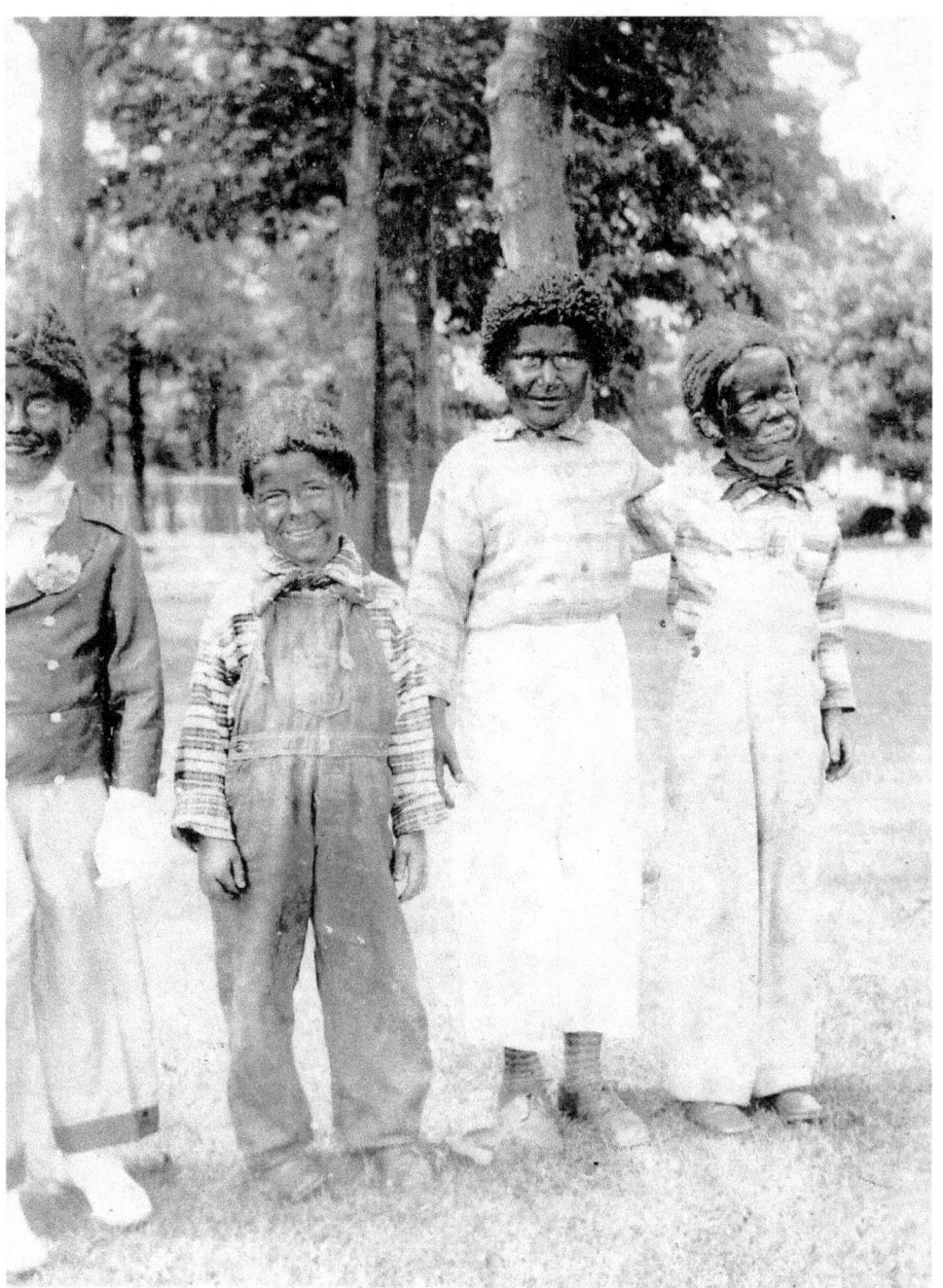

1920

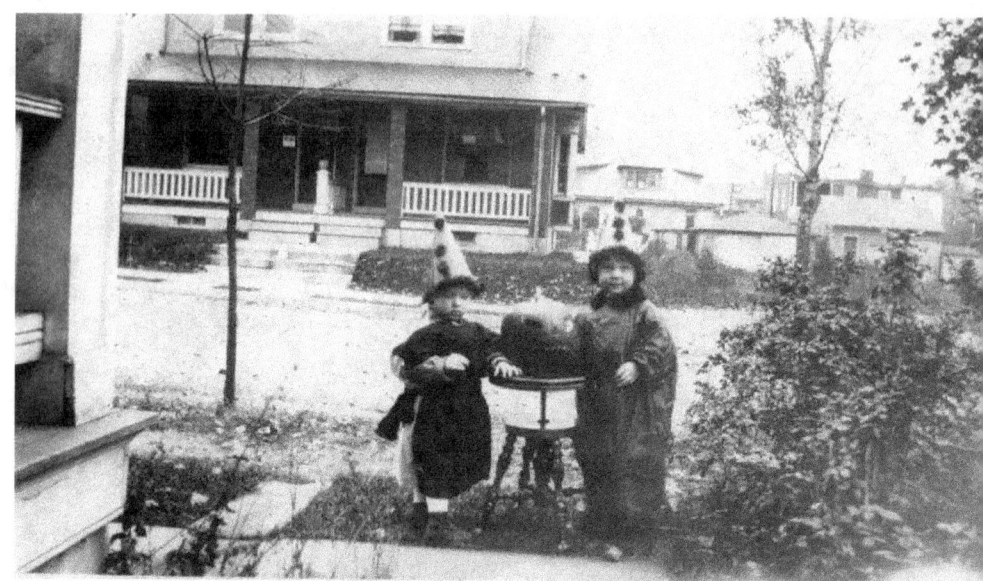

1926 ABOVE / 1932 BELOW

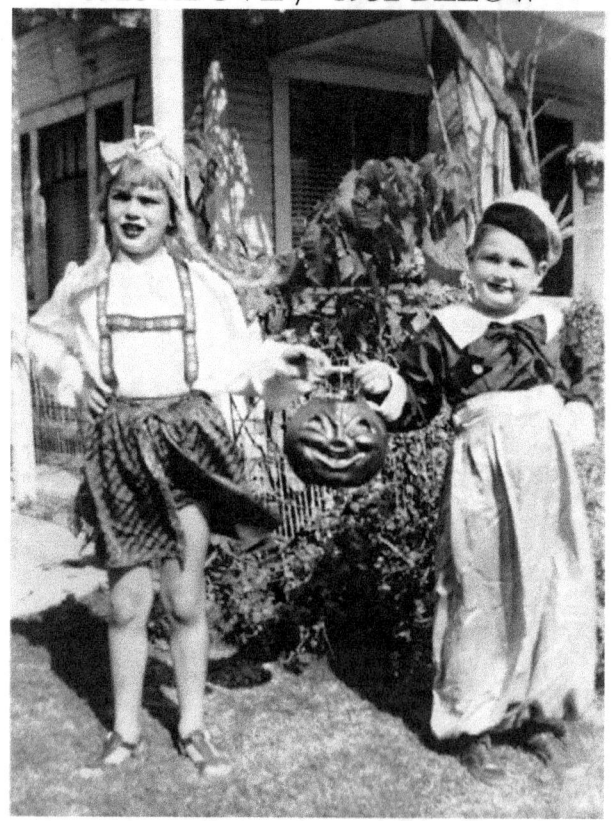

Vintage Halloween Photos

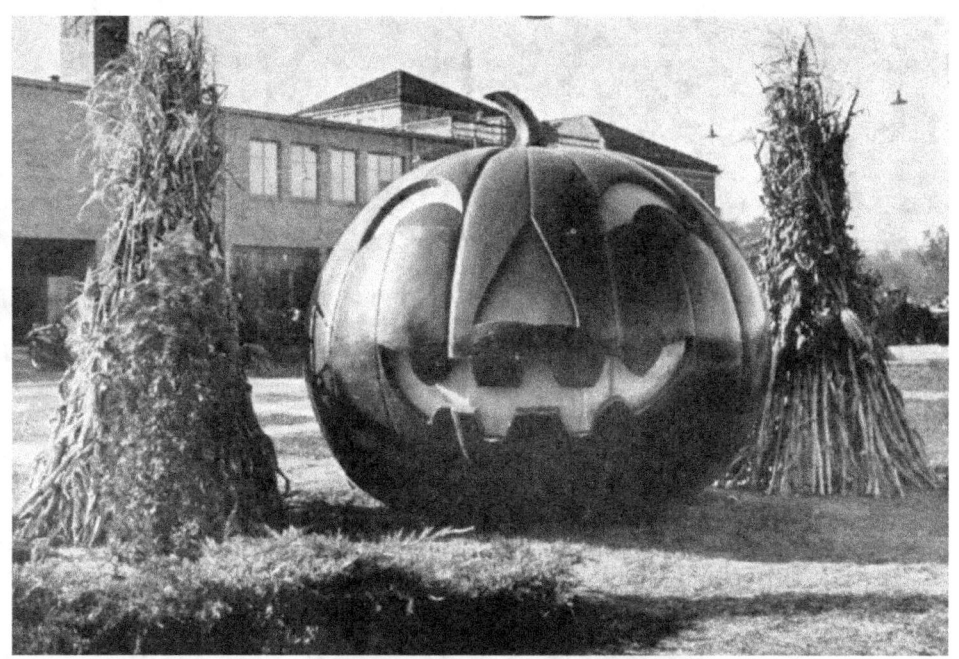

1933 ABOVE / 1944 BELOW

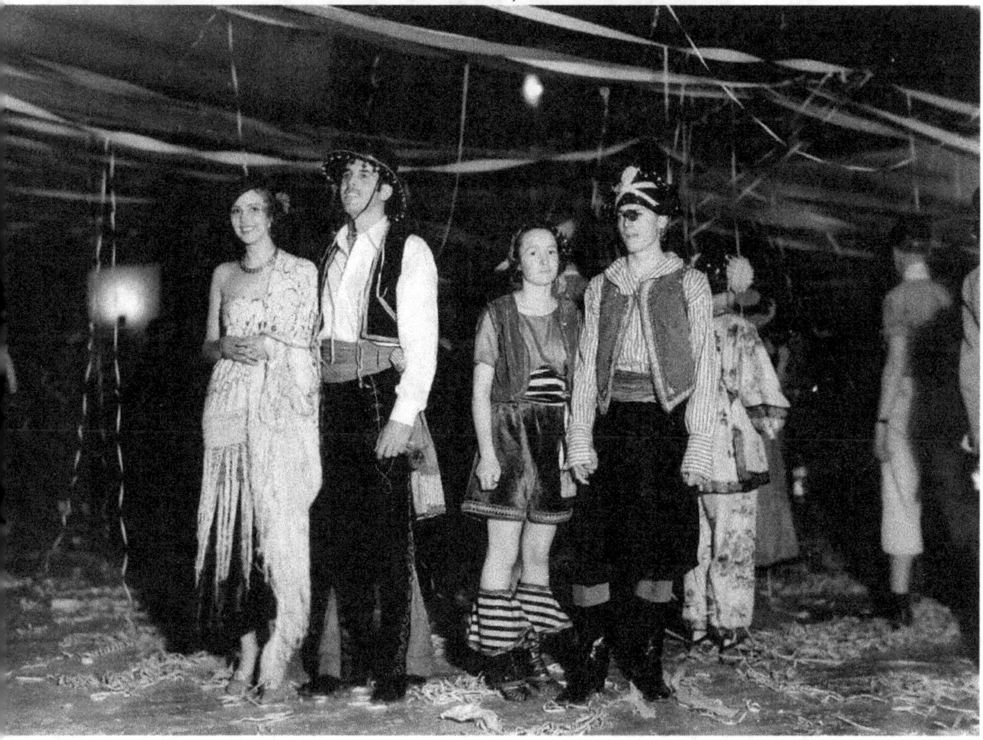

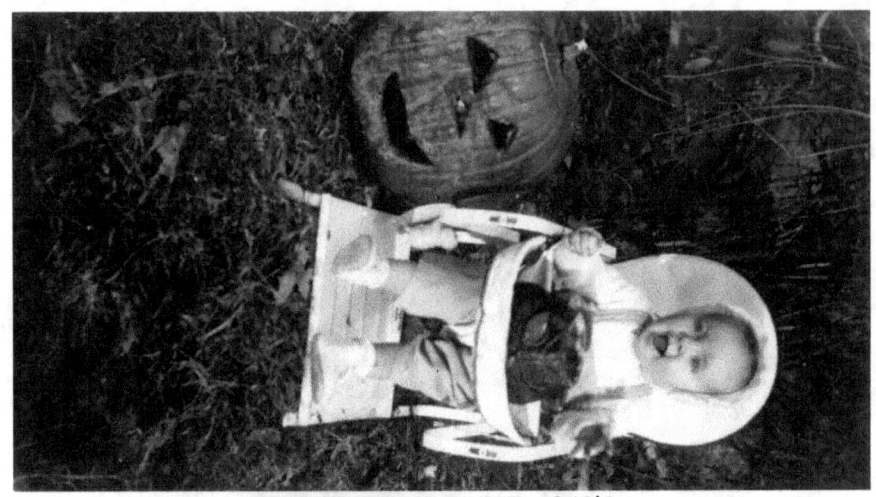

BOTH FROM THE 1940'S

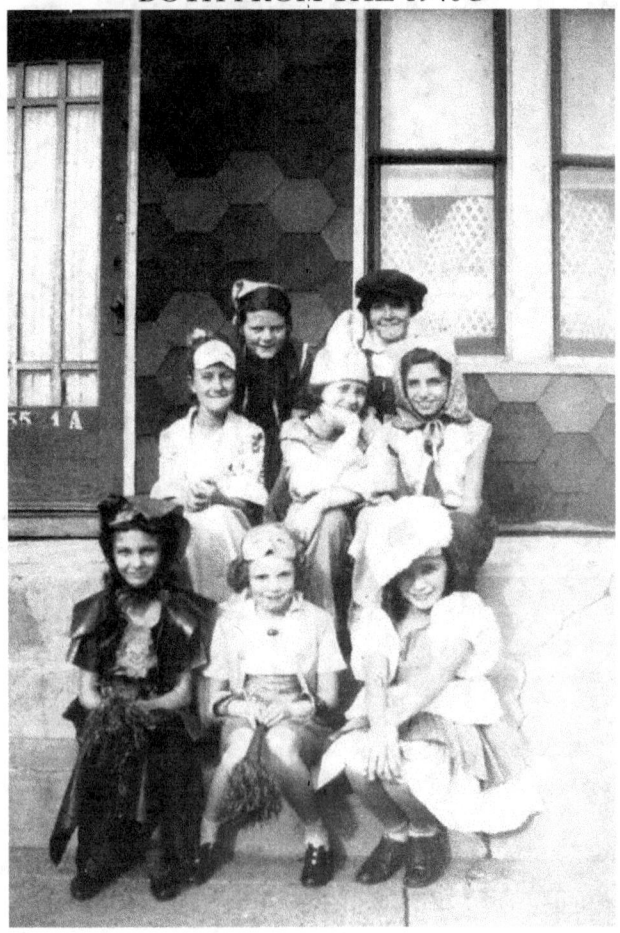

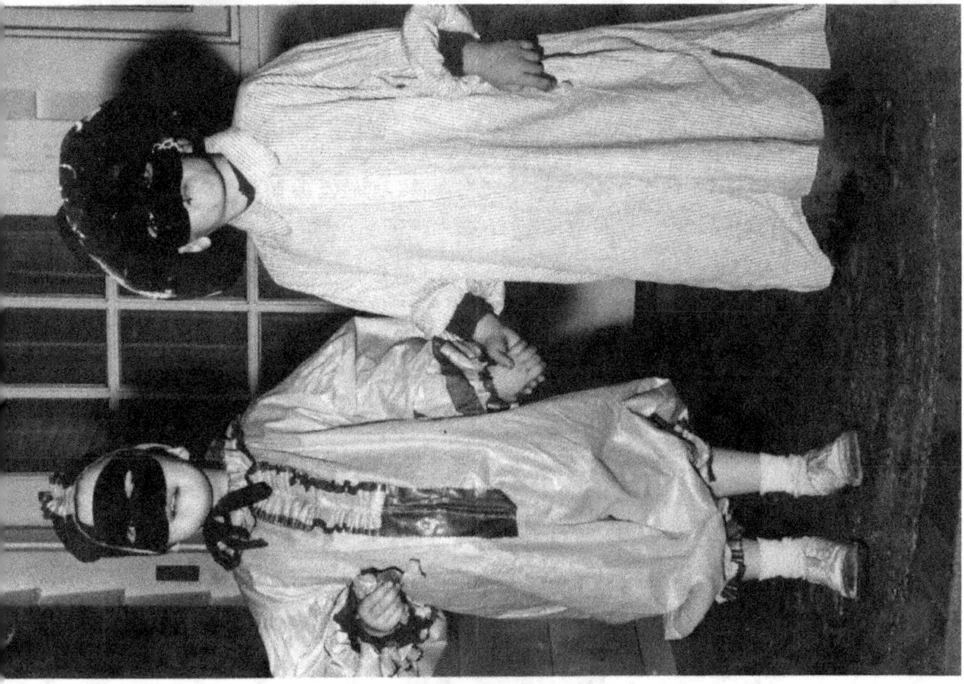

Vintage Halloween Photos

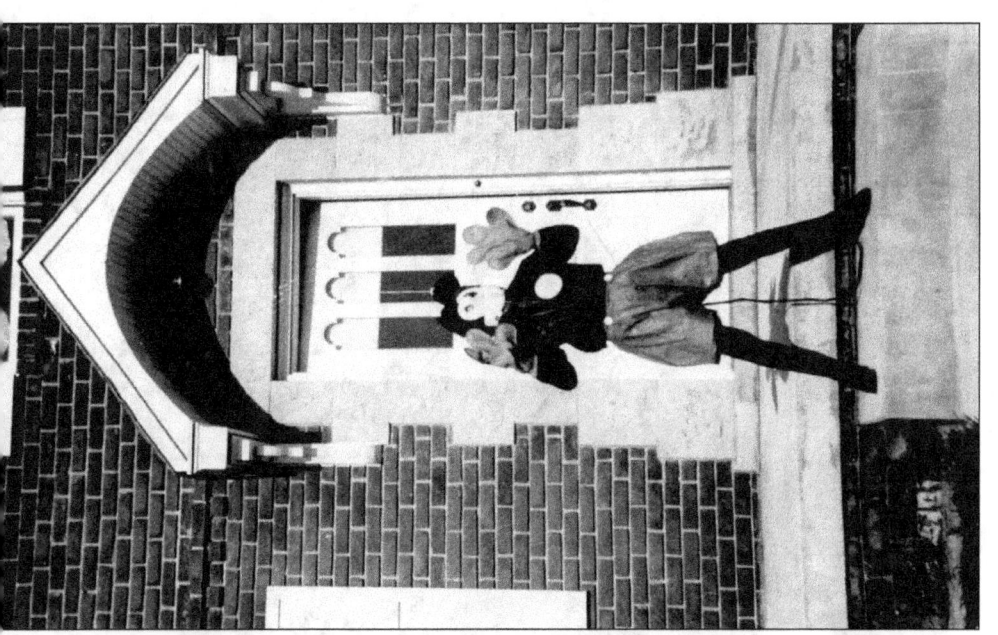

BOTH 1940'S

BOTH 1947

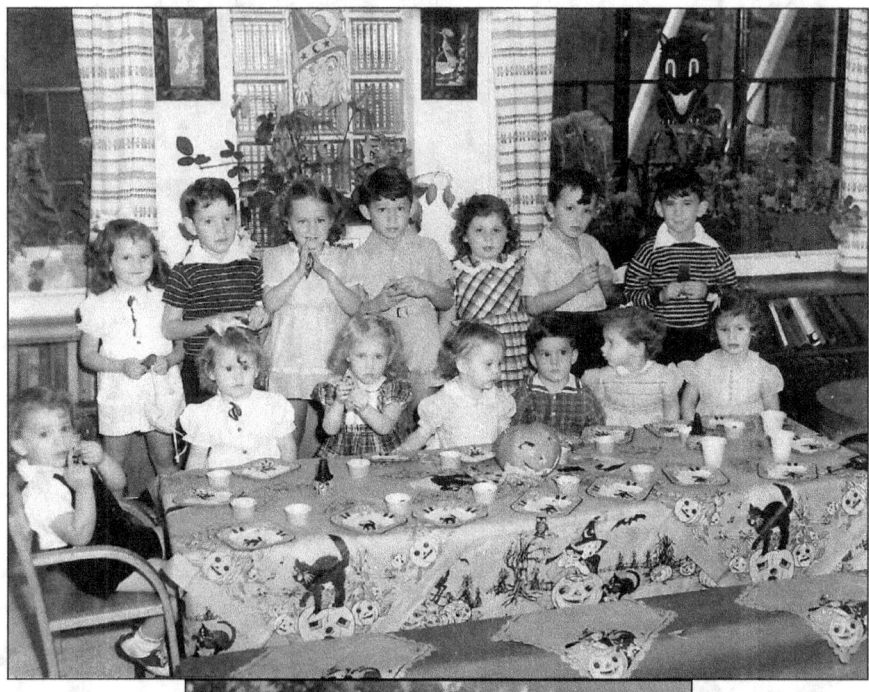

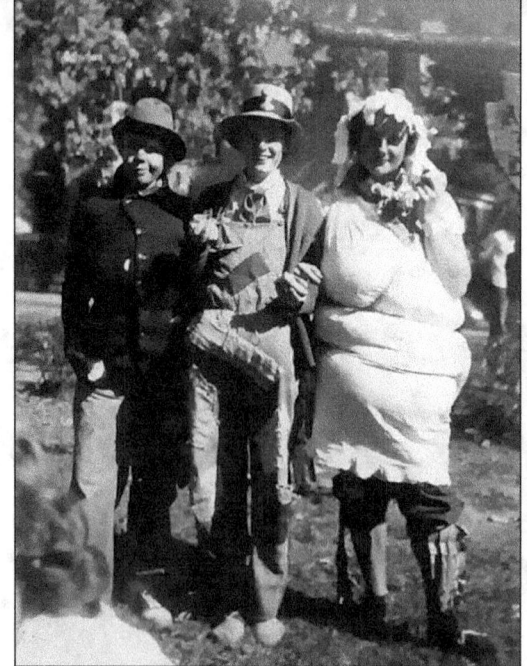

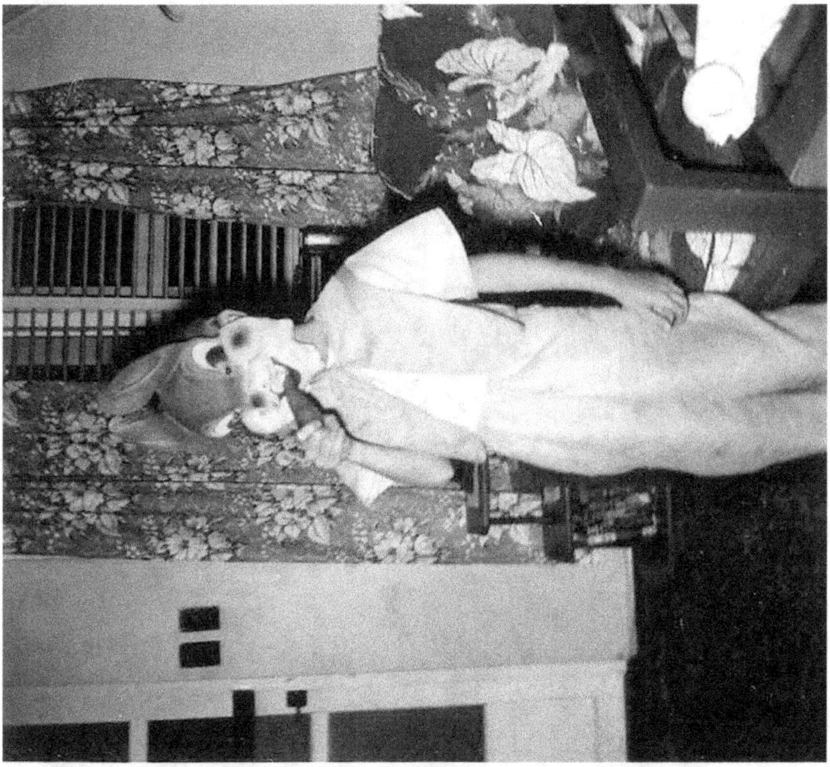

Vintage Halloween Photos

ABOVE 1949 / BELOW 1956

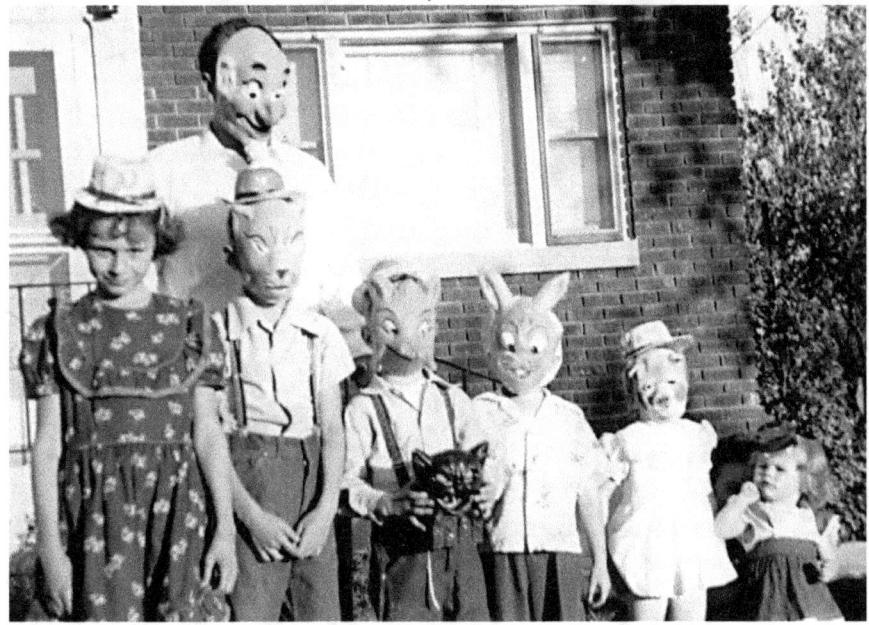

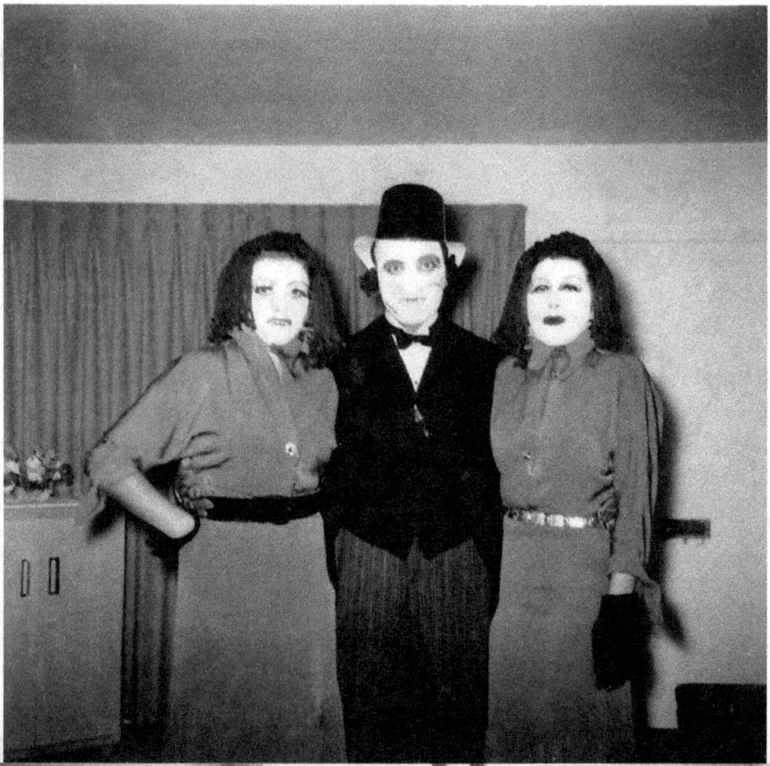

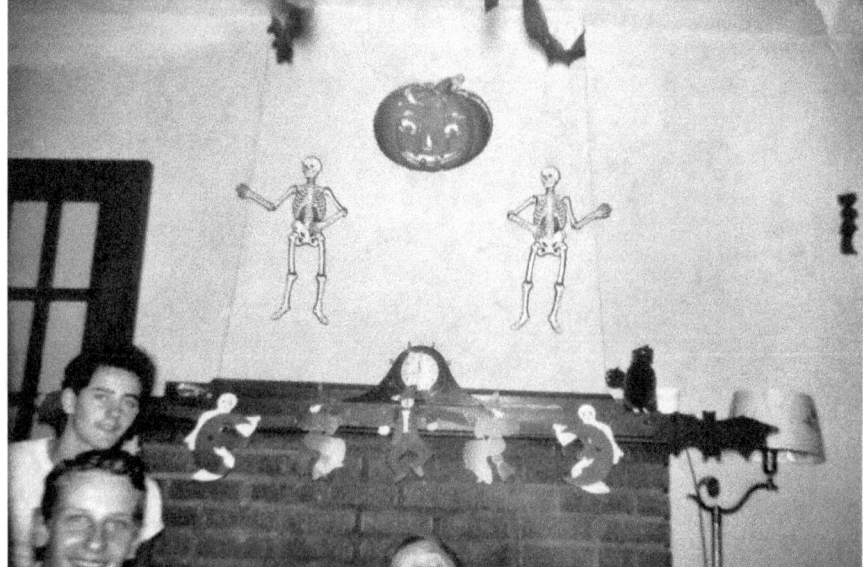

BOTH 1950'S

Vintage Halloween Photos

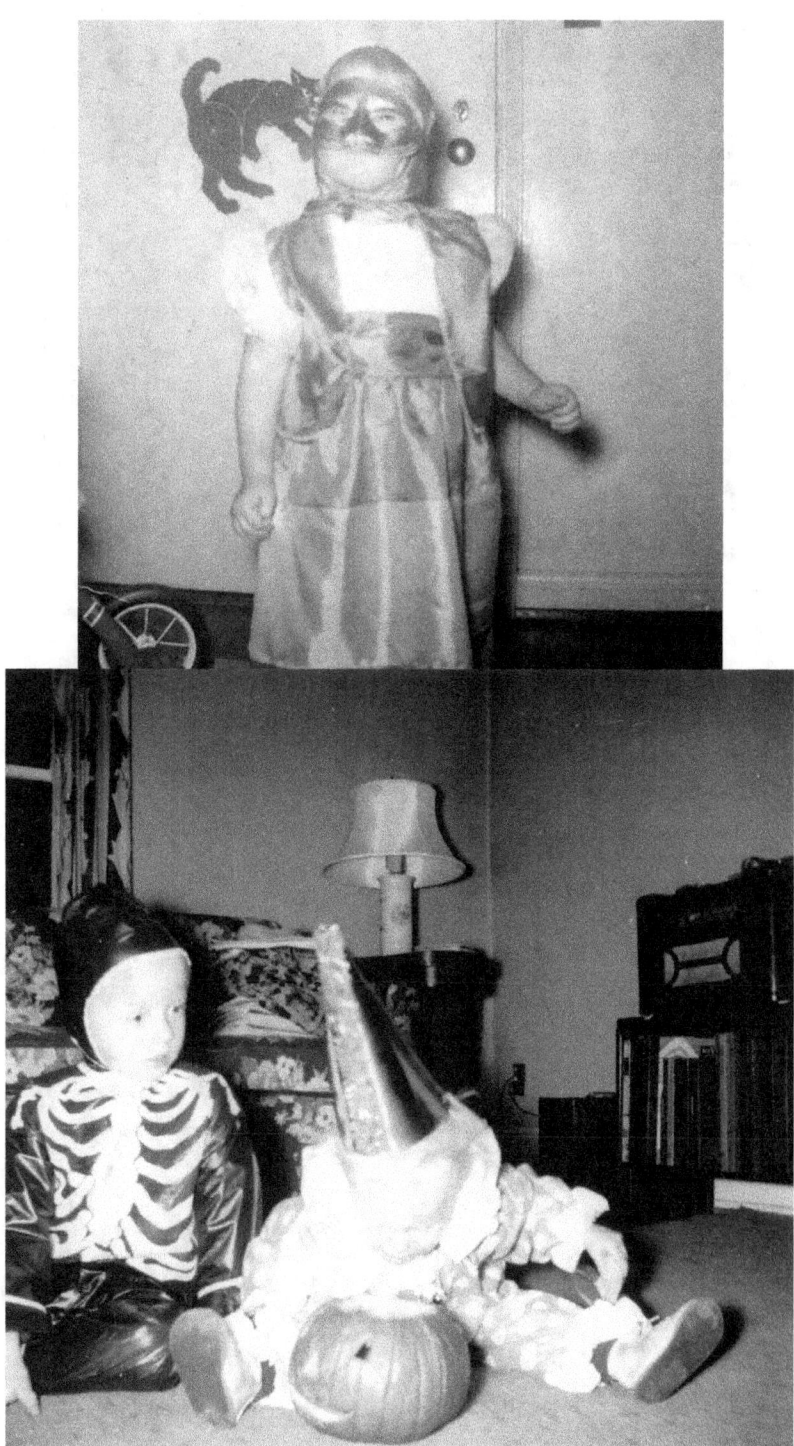

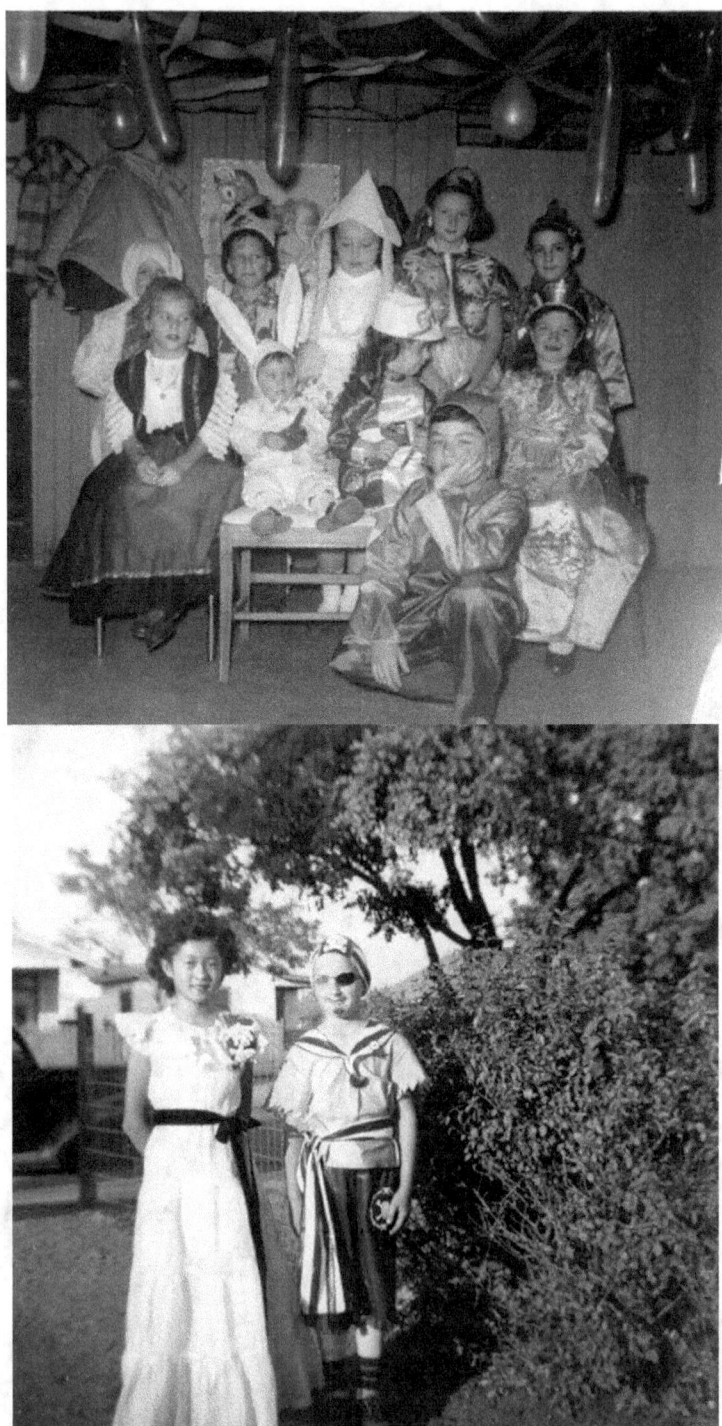

Vintage Halloween Photos

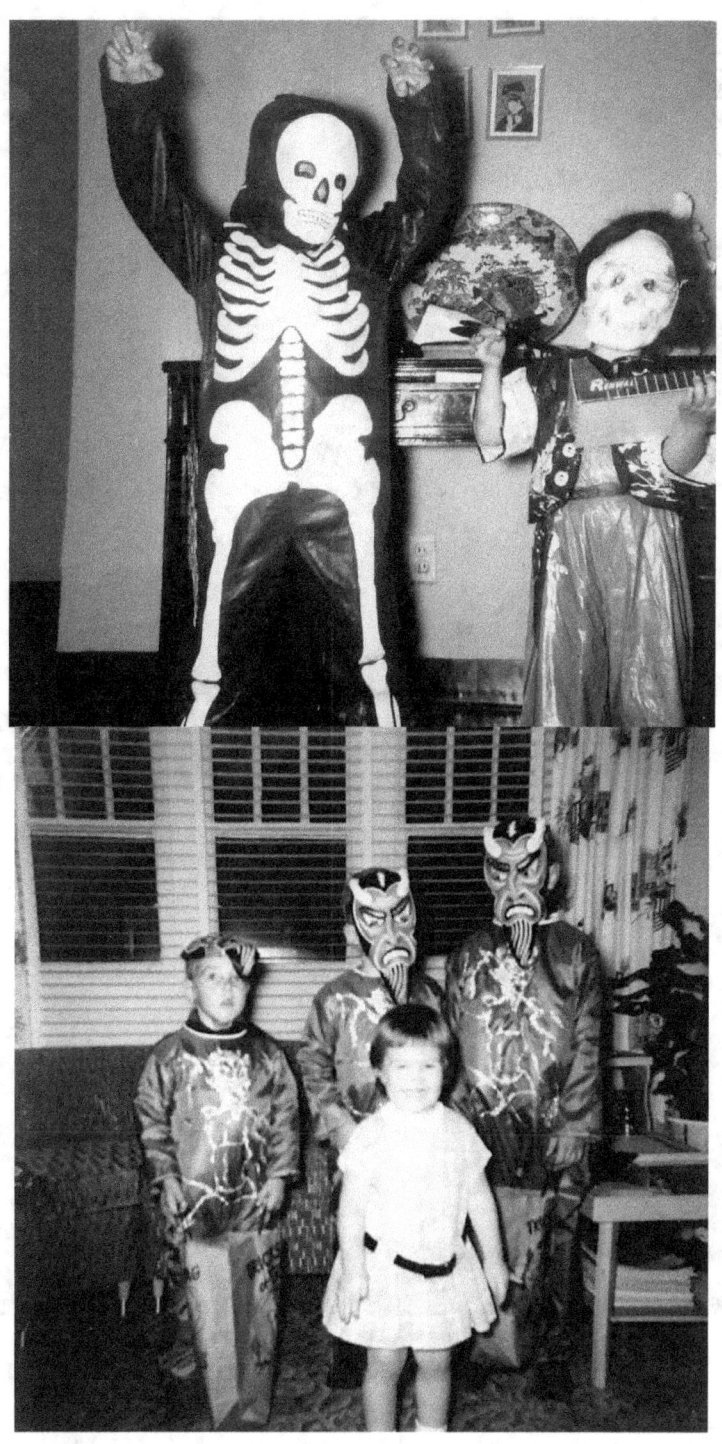

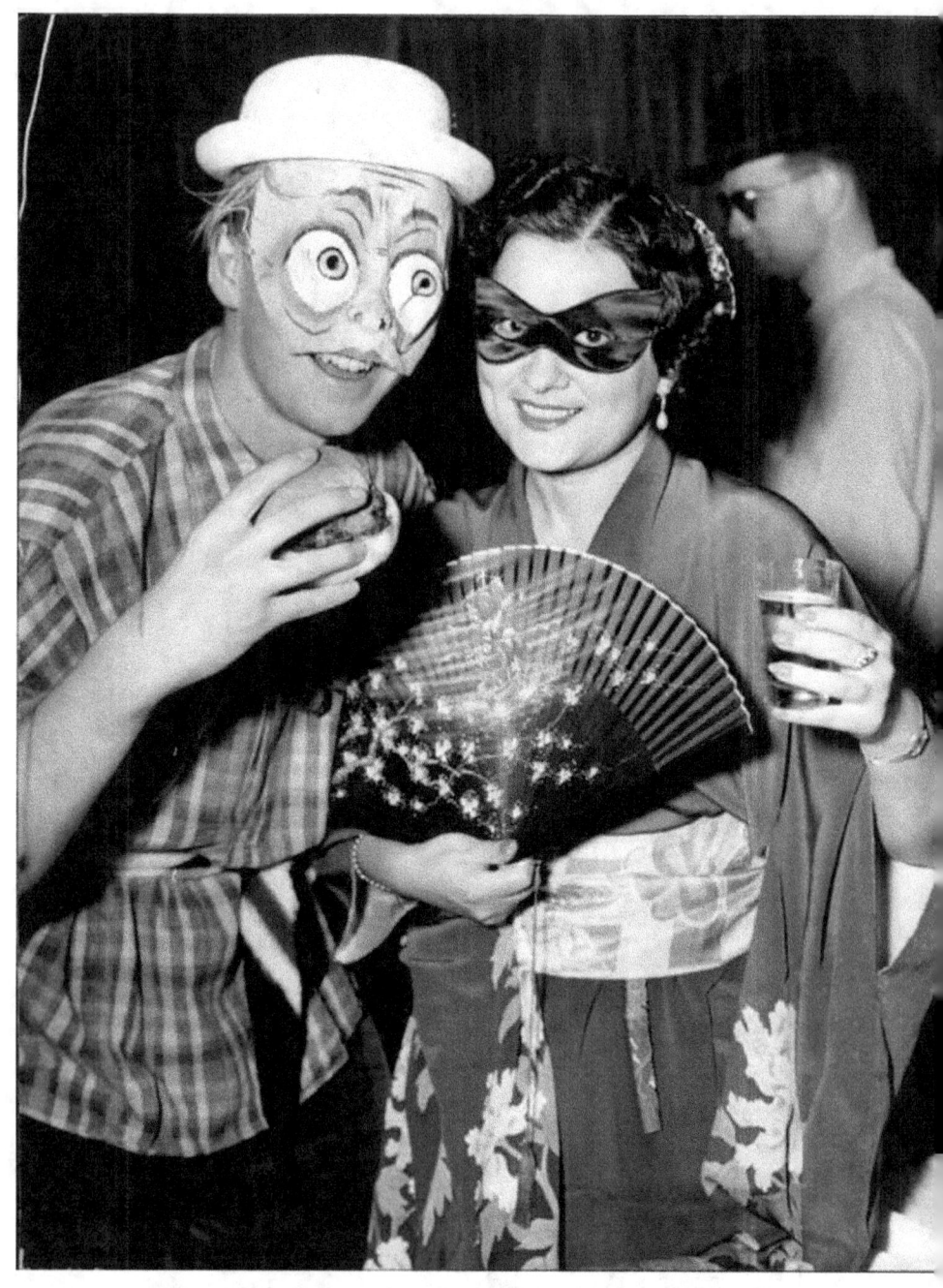

1951

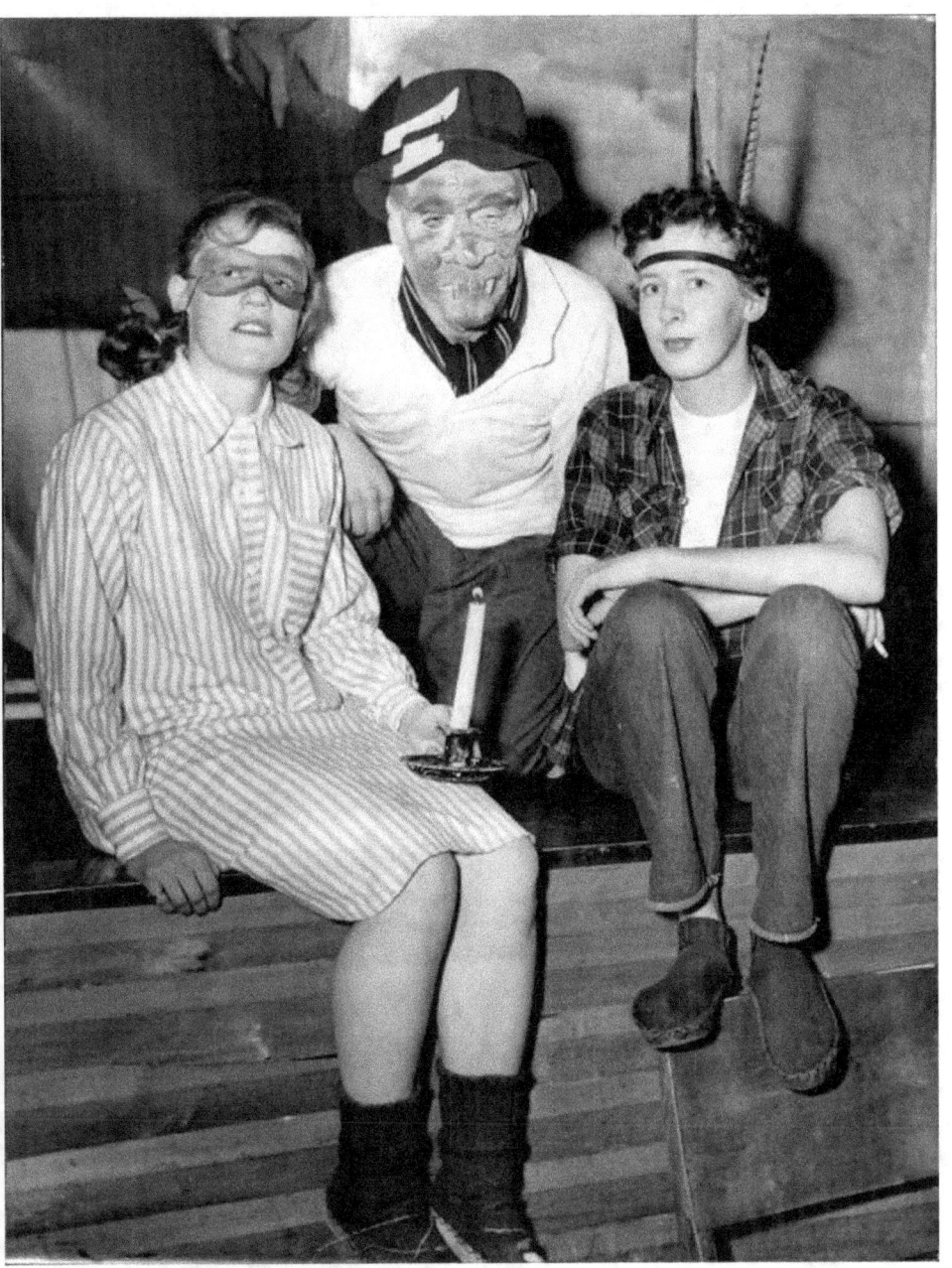

1951

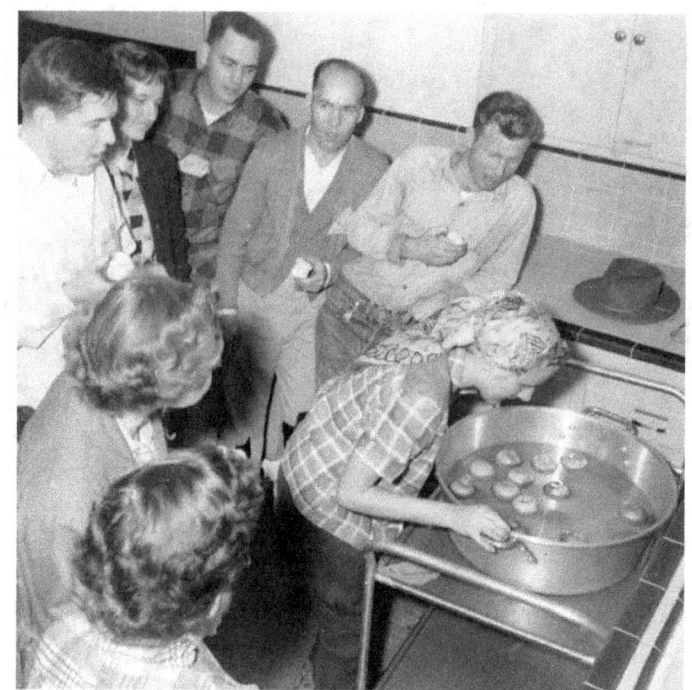

1952 ABOVE / 1960 BELOW

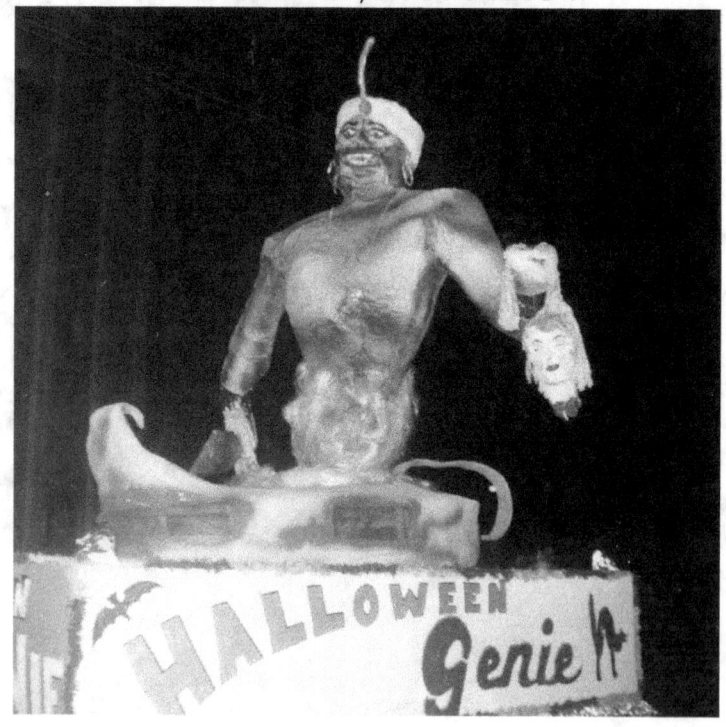

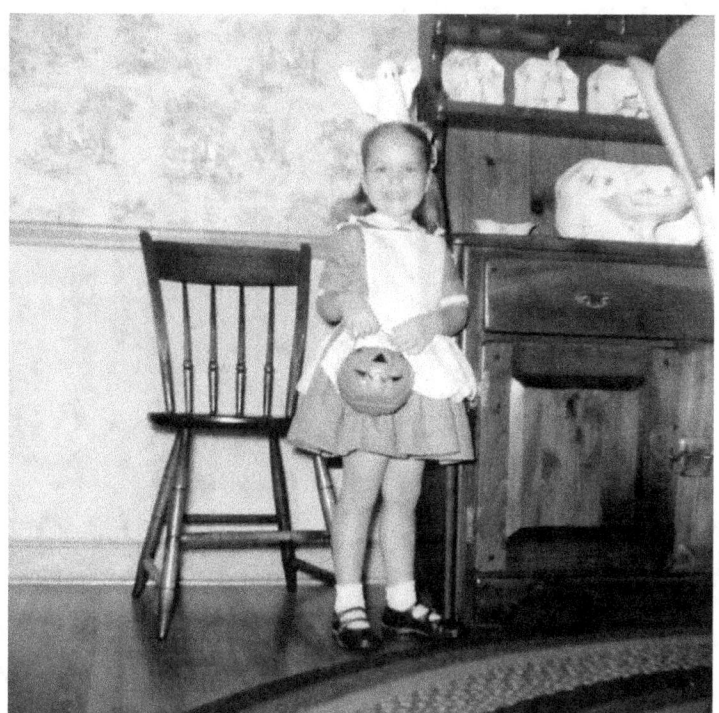

BOTH 1960

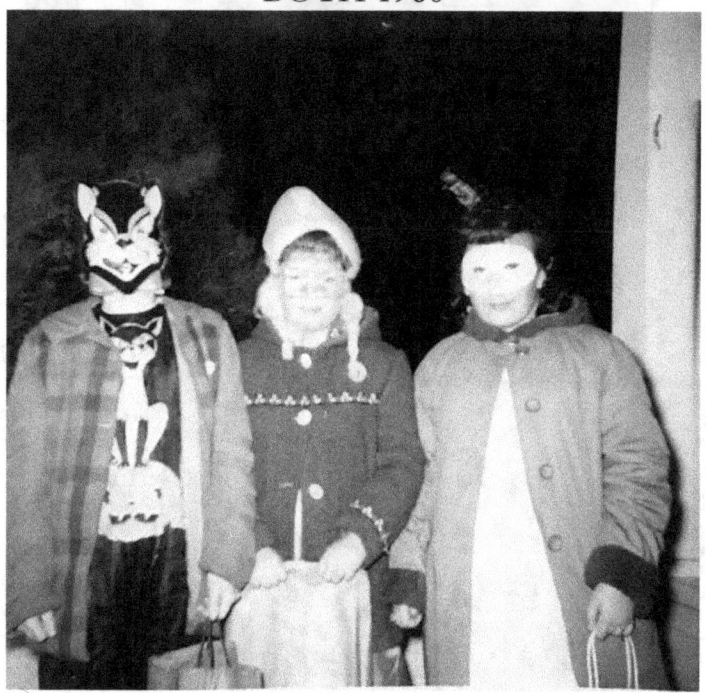

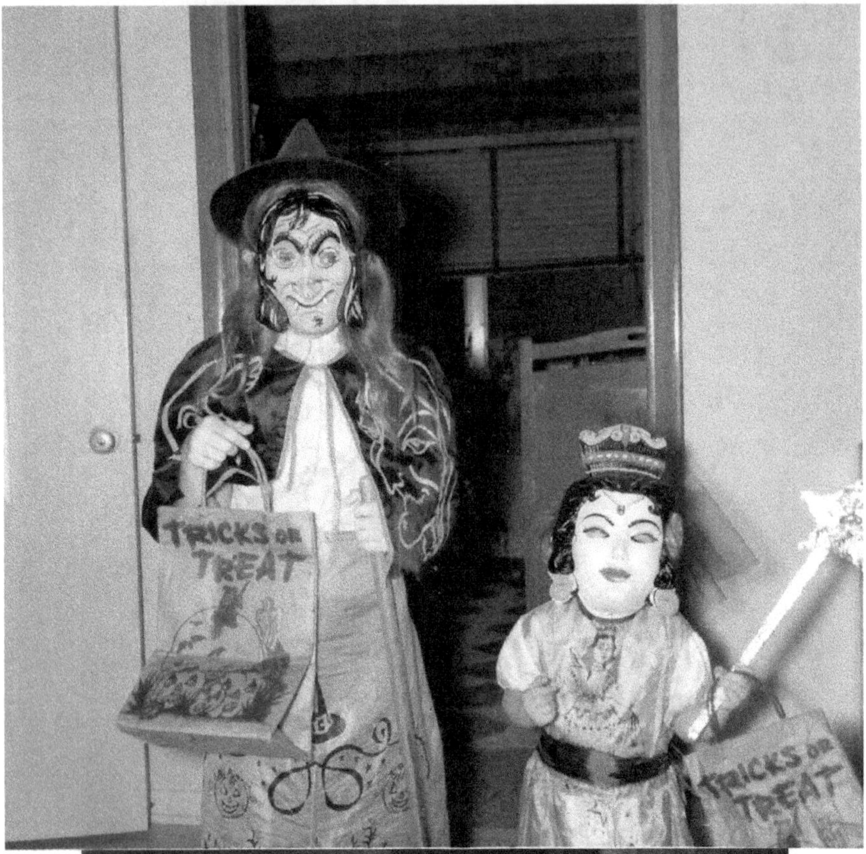

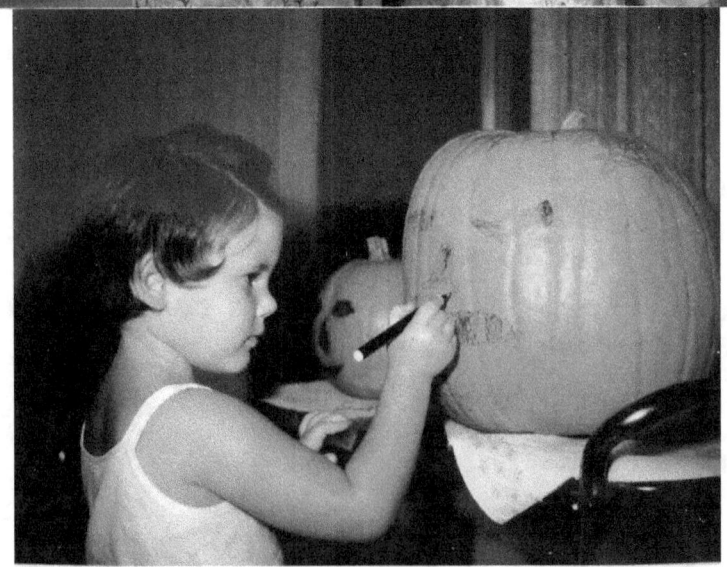

Vintage Halloween Photos

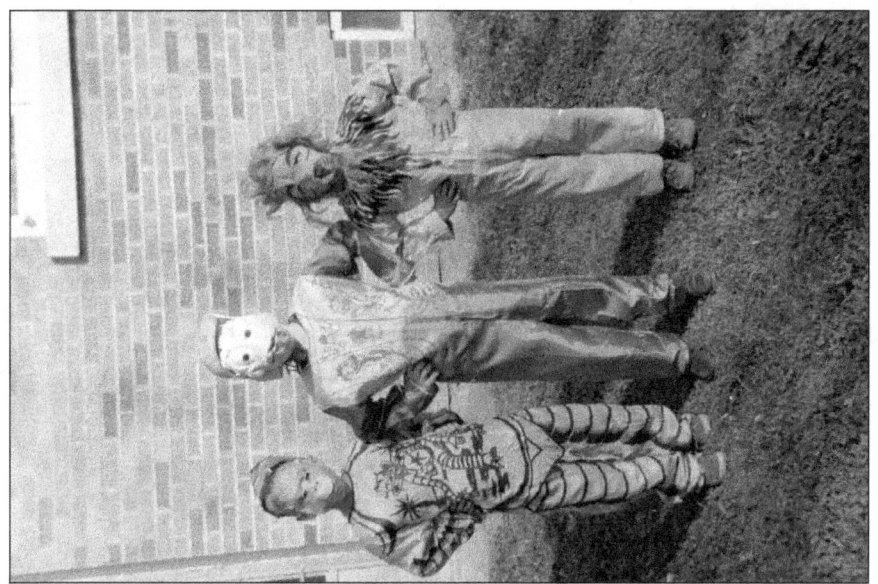

1960'S

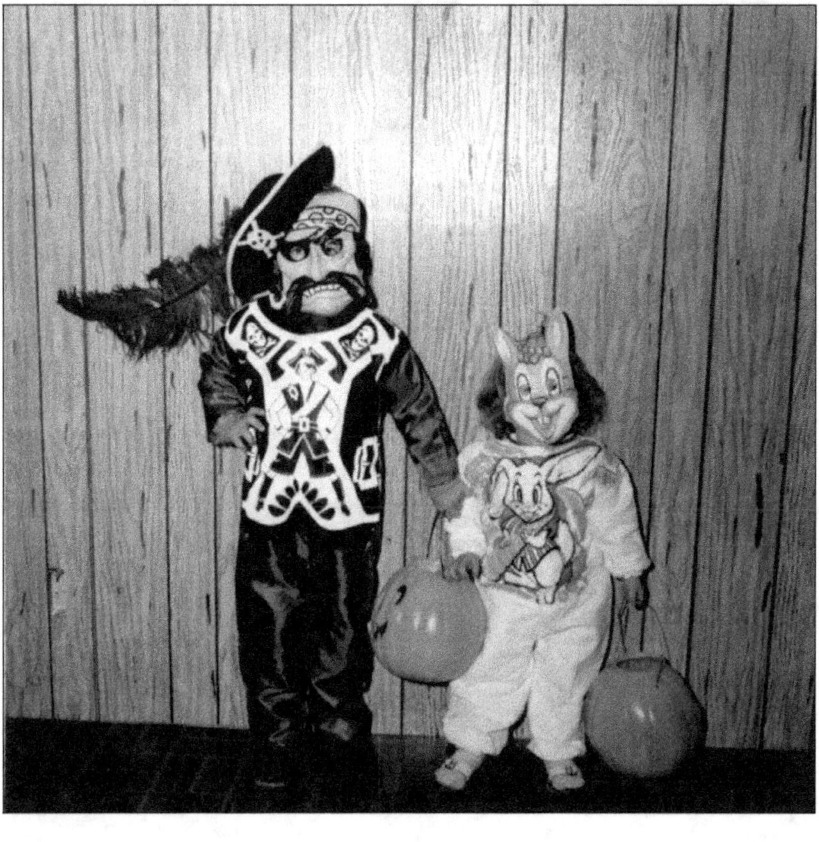

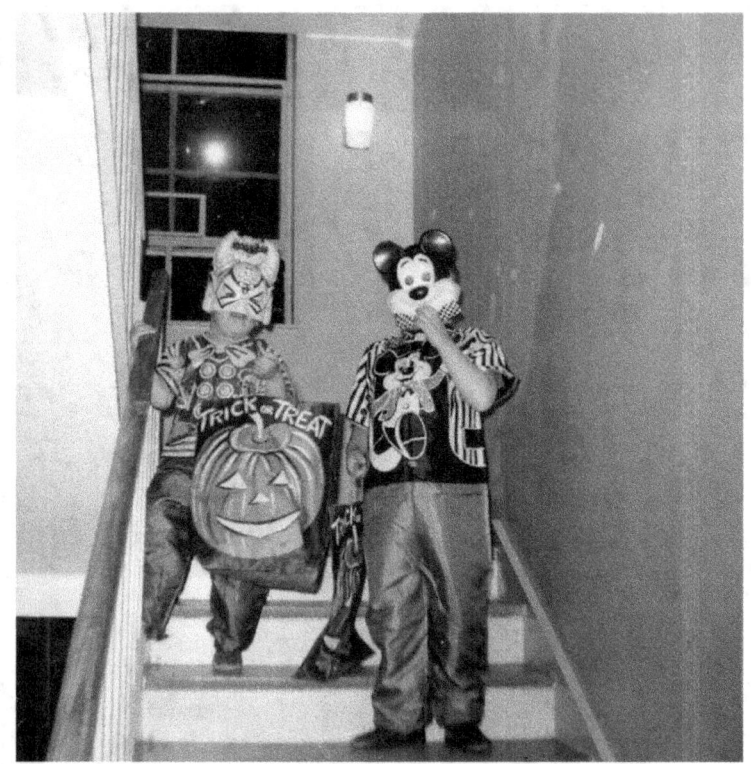

1963 ABOVE / 1966 BELOW

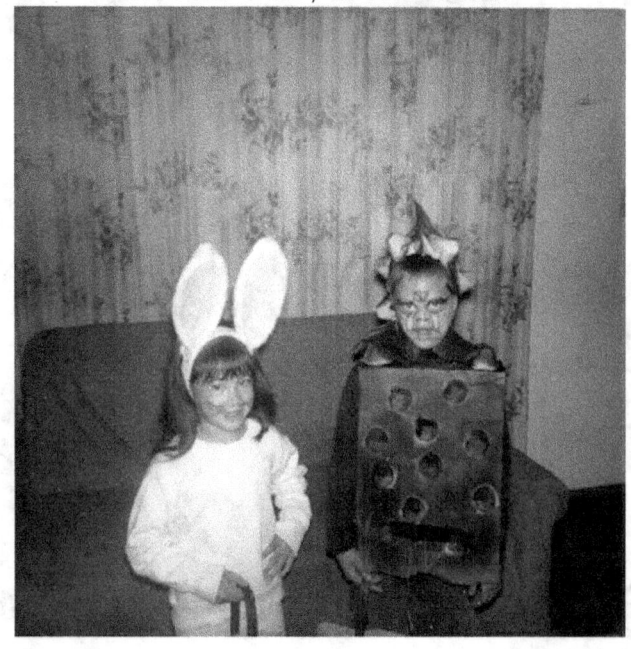

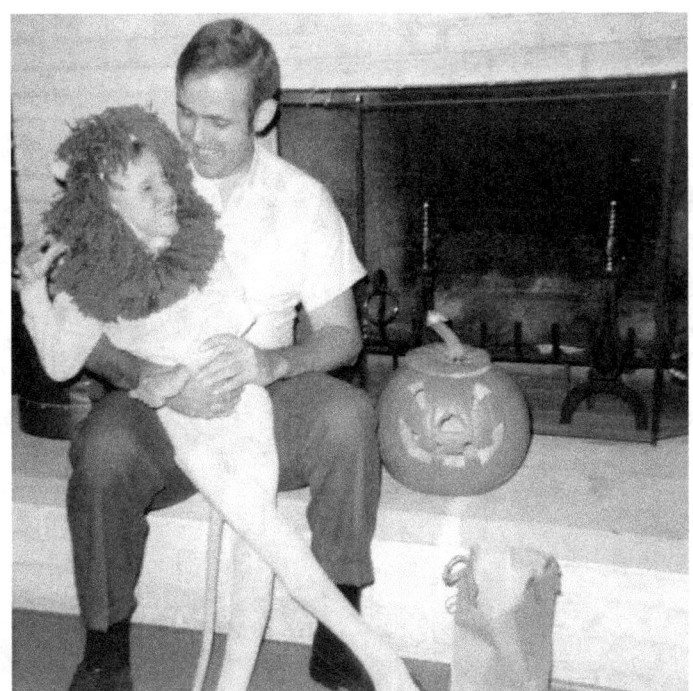

1970'S

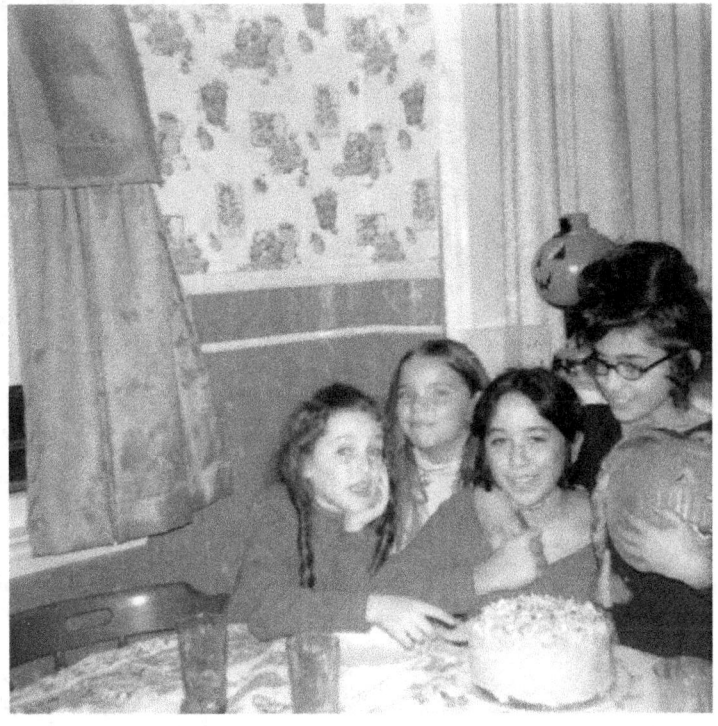

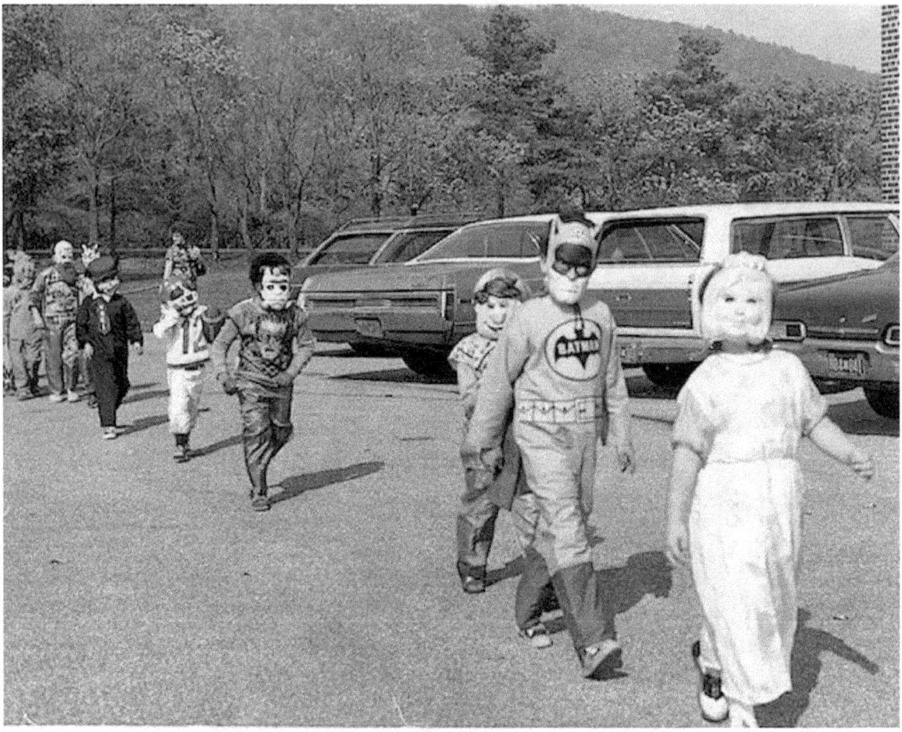

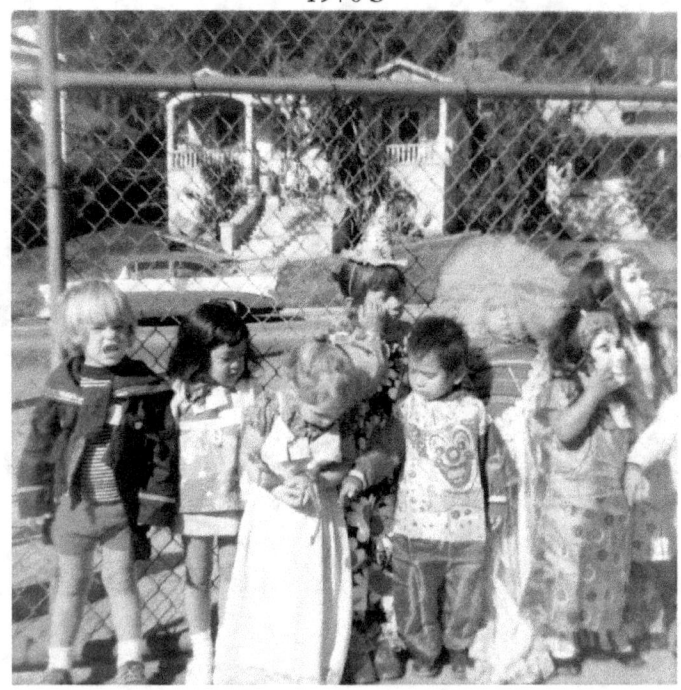

1970'S

Vintage Halloween Photos

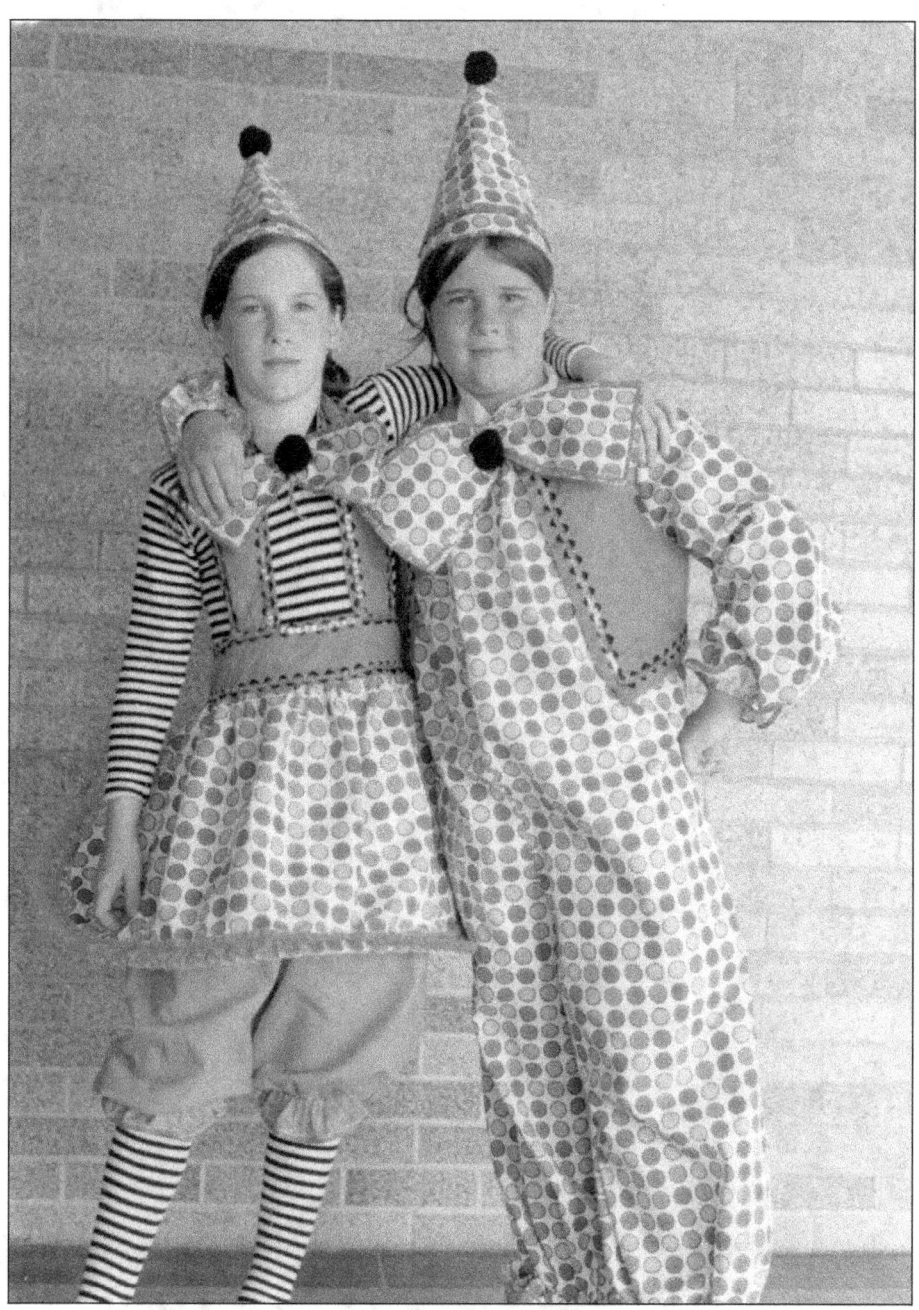

1972

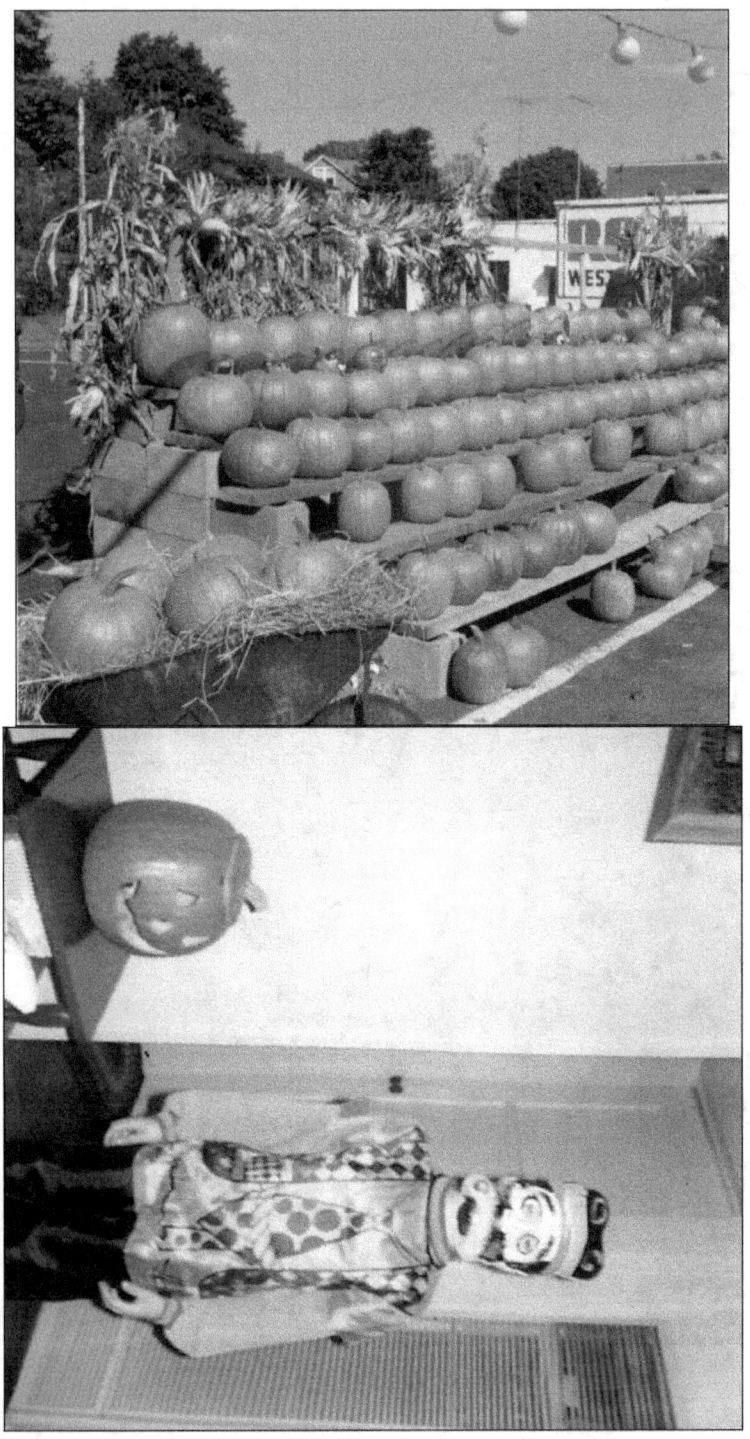

1984

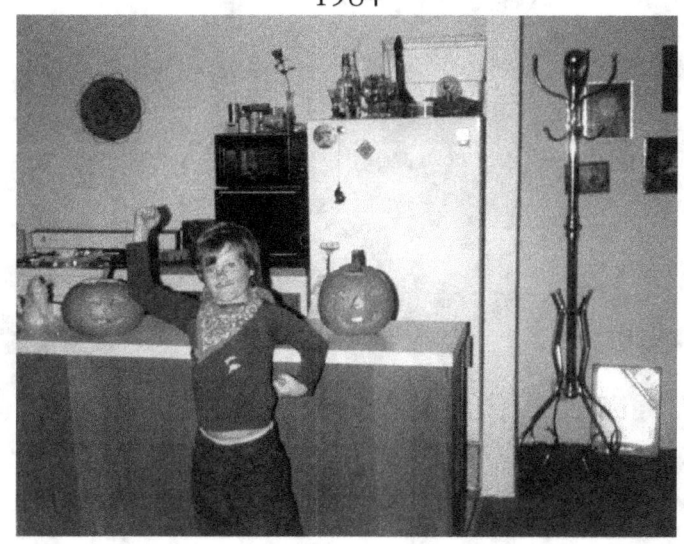

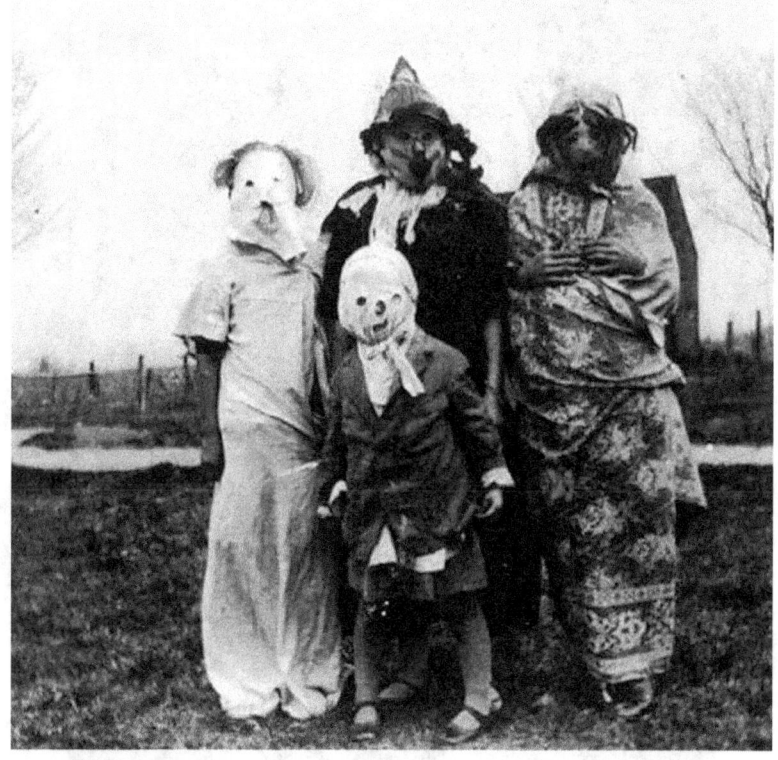

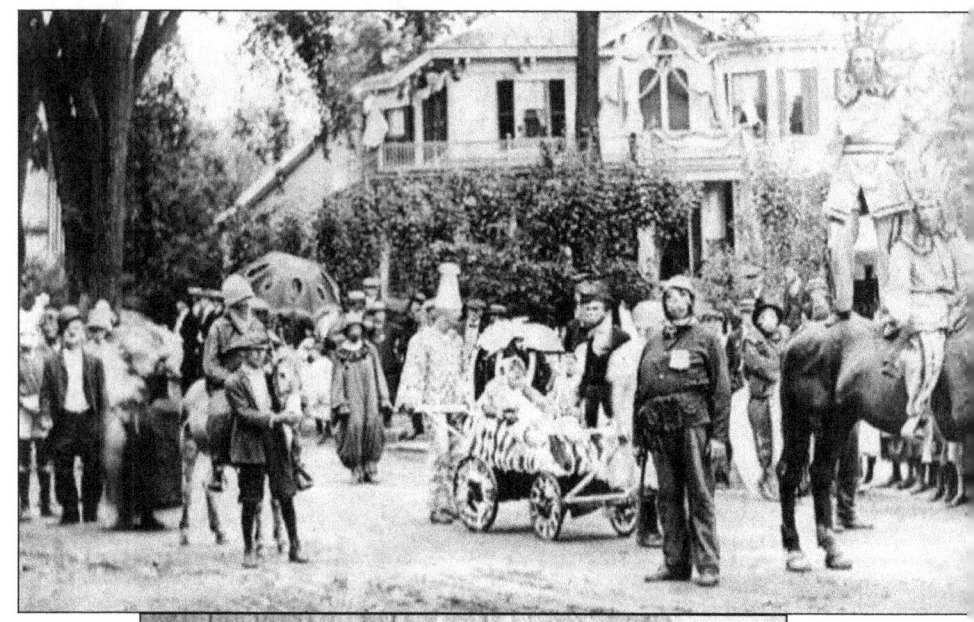

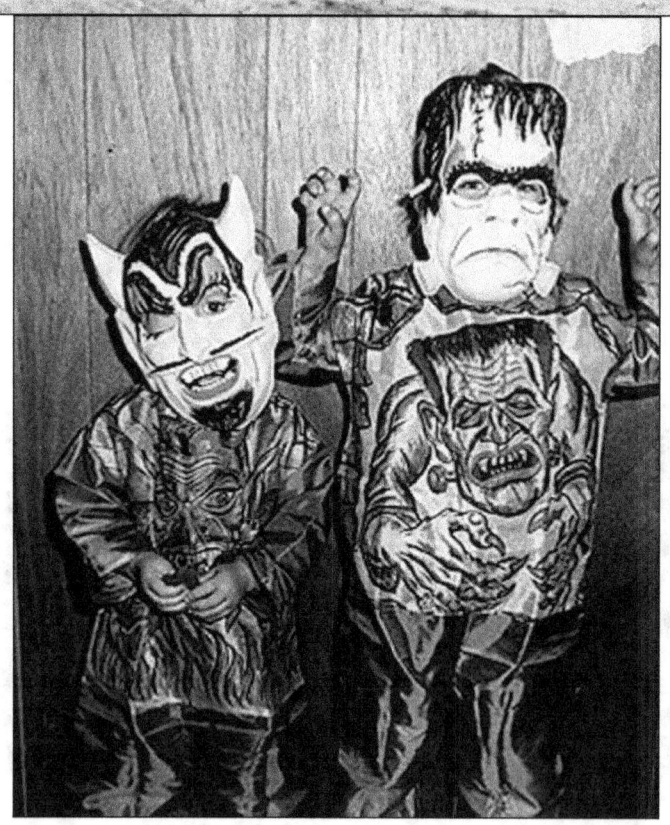

Vintage Halloween Photos

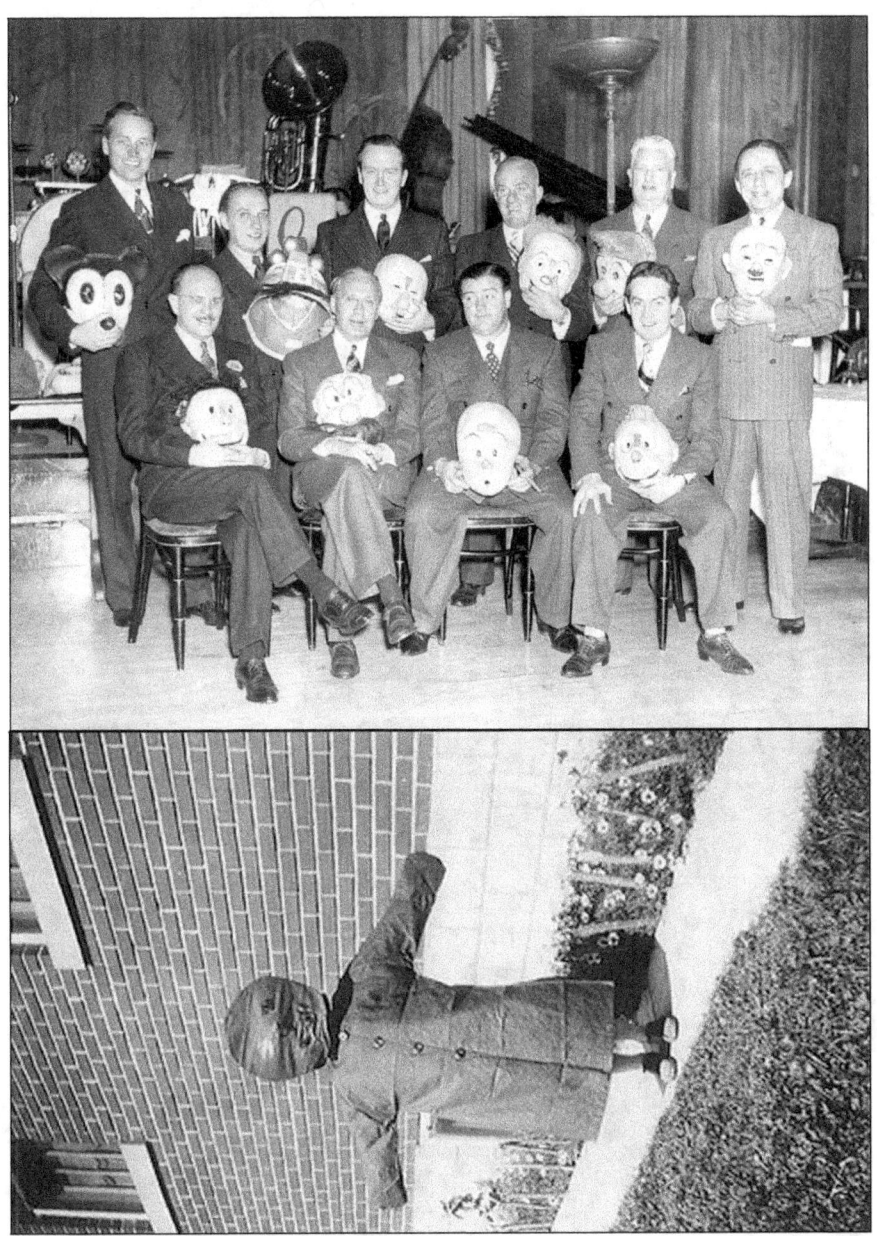

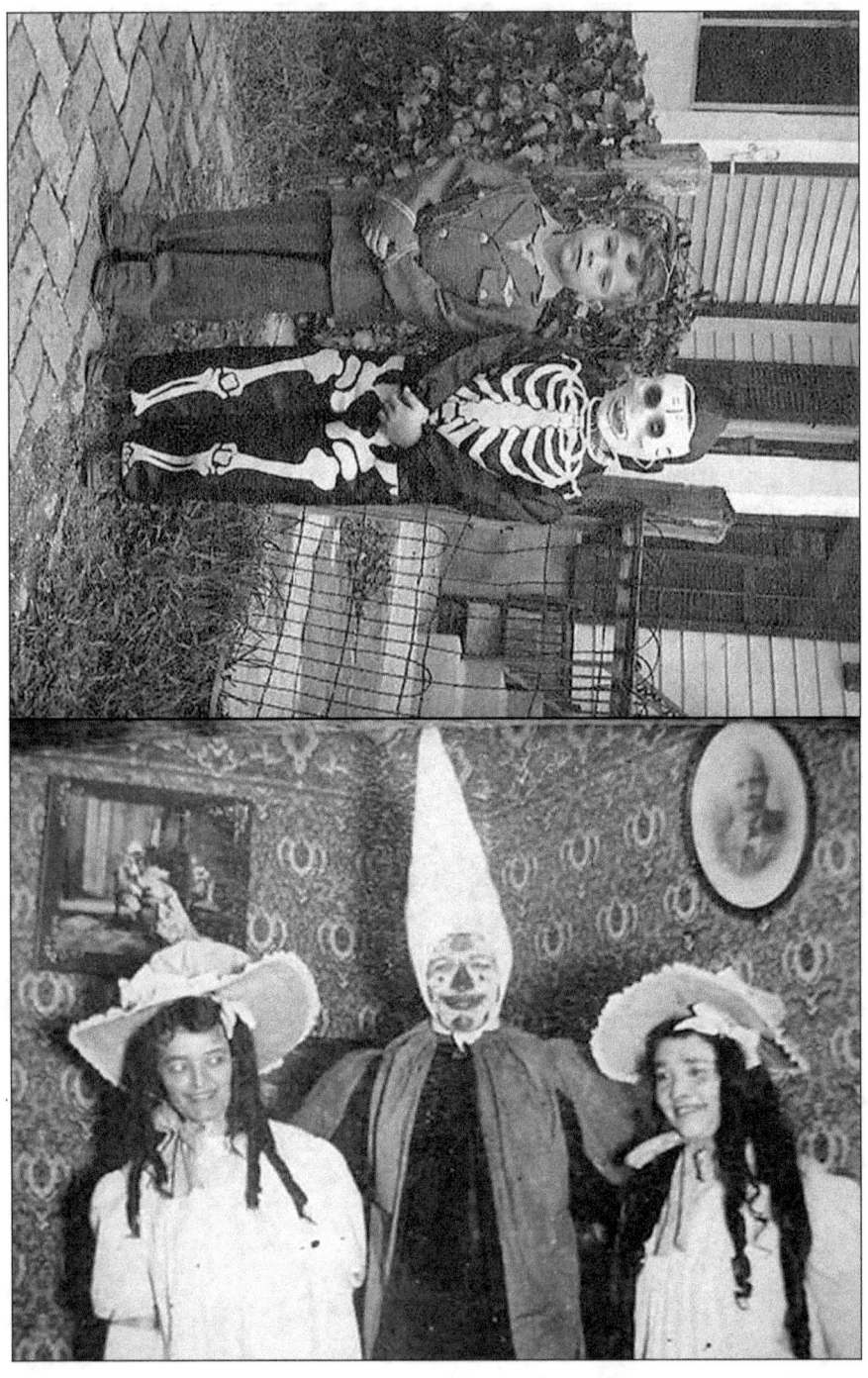

Vintage Halloween Photos

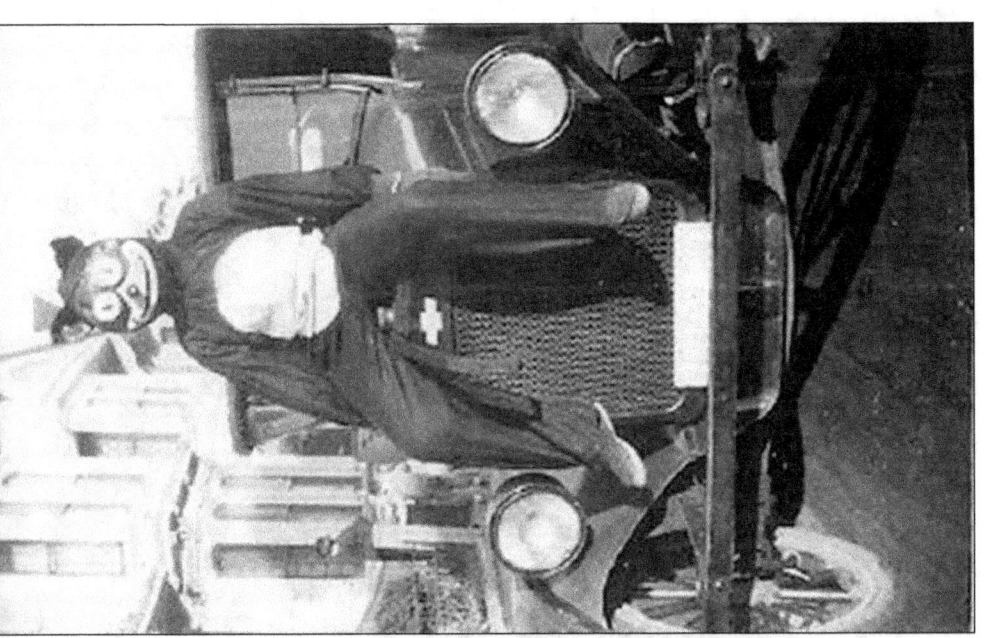

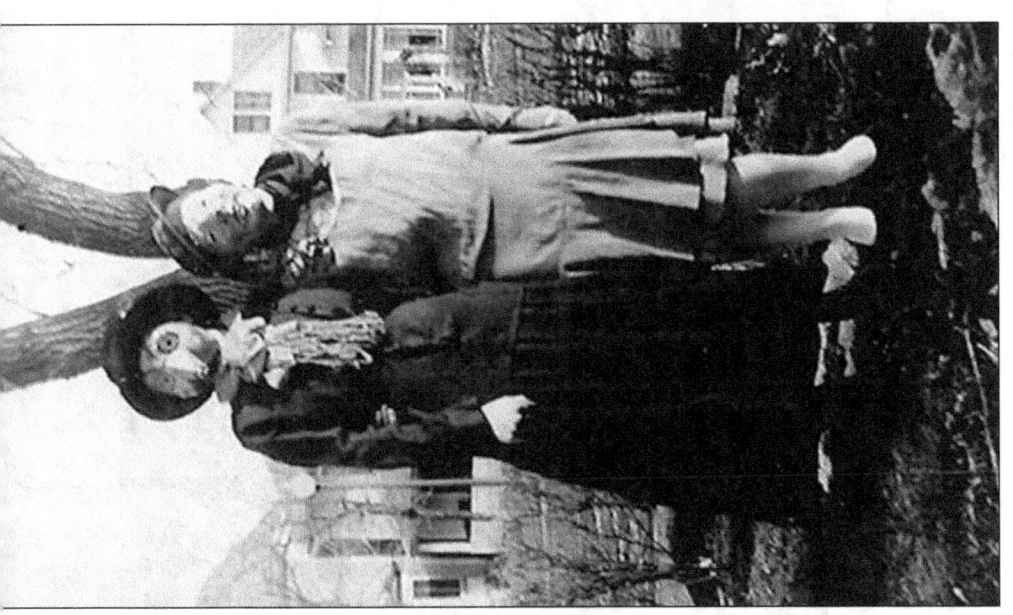

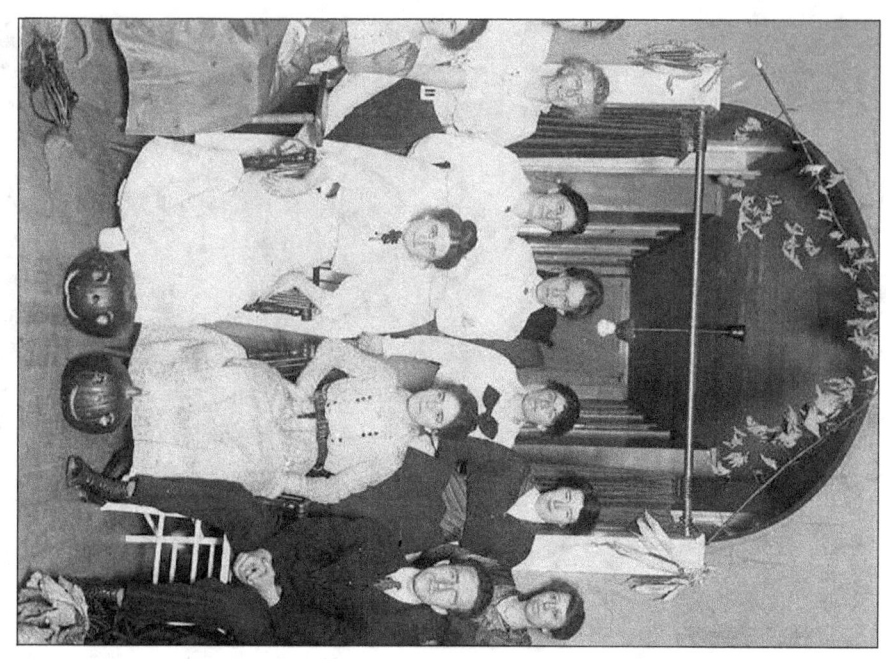

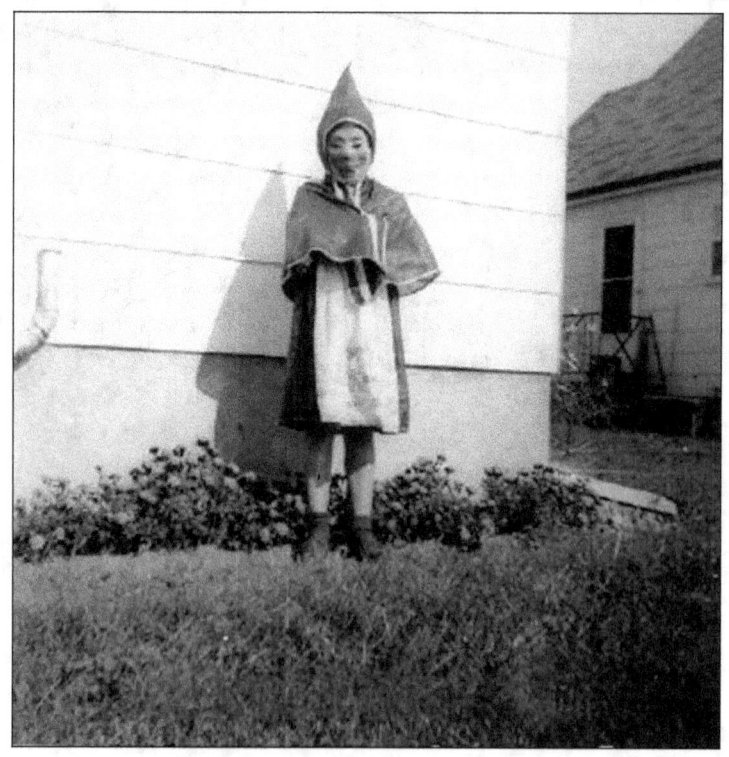

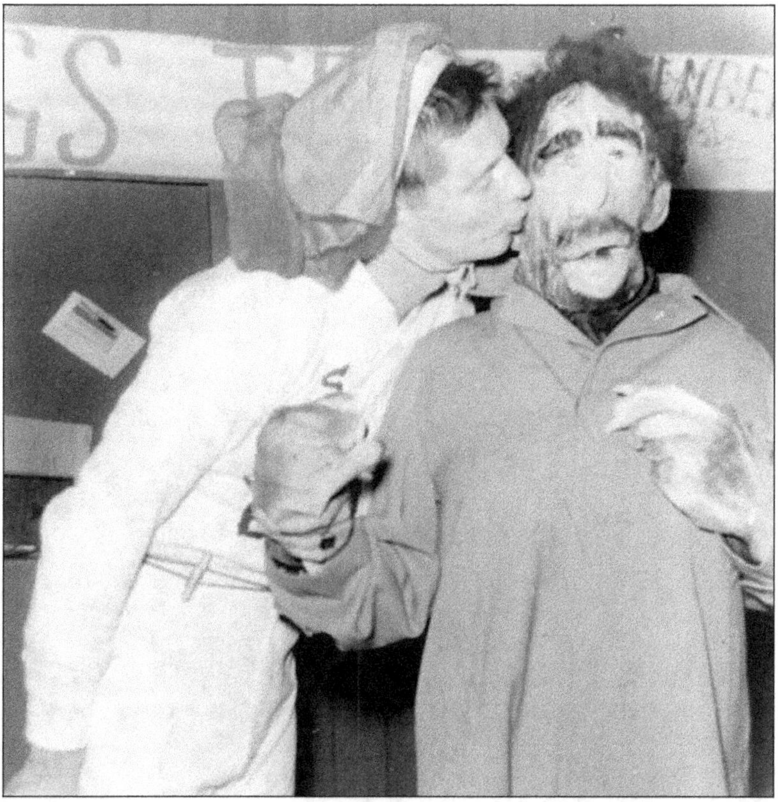

Vintage Halloween Photos

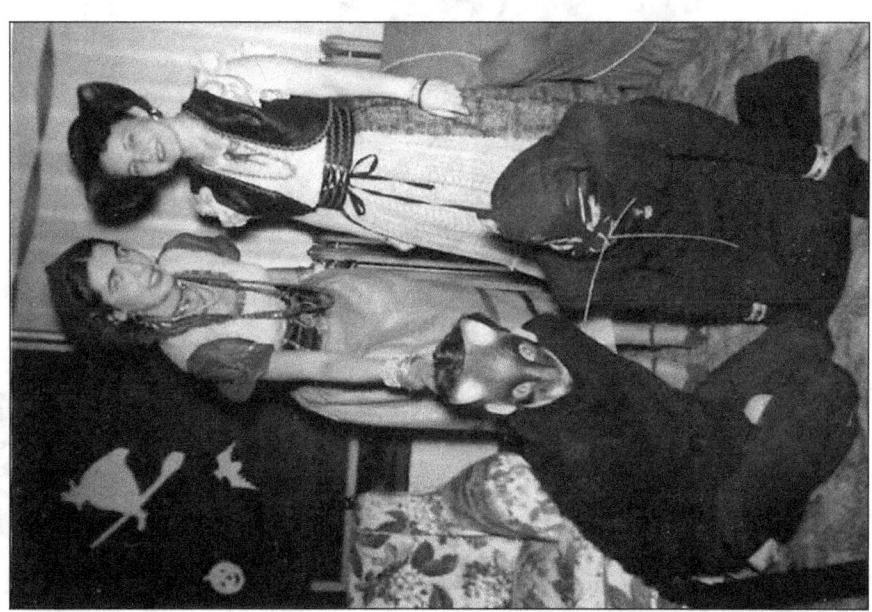

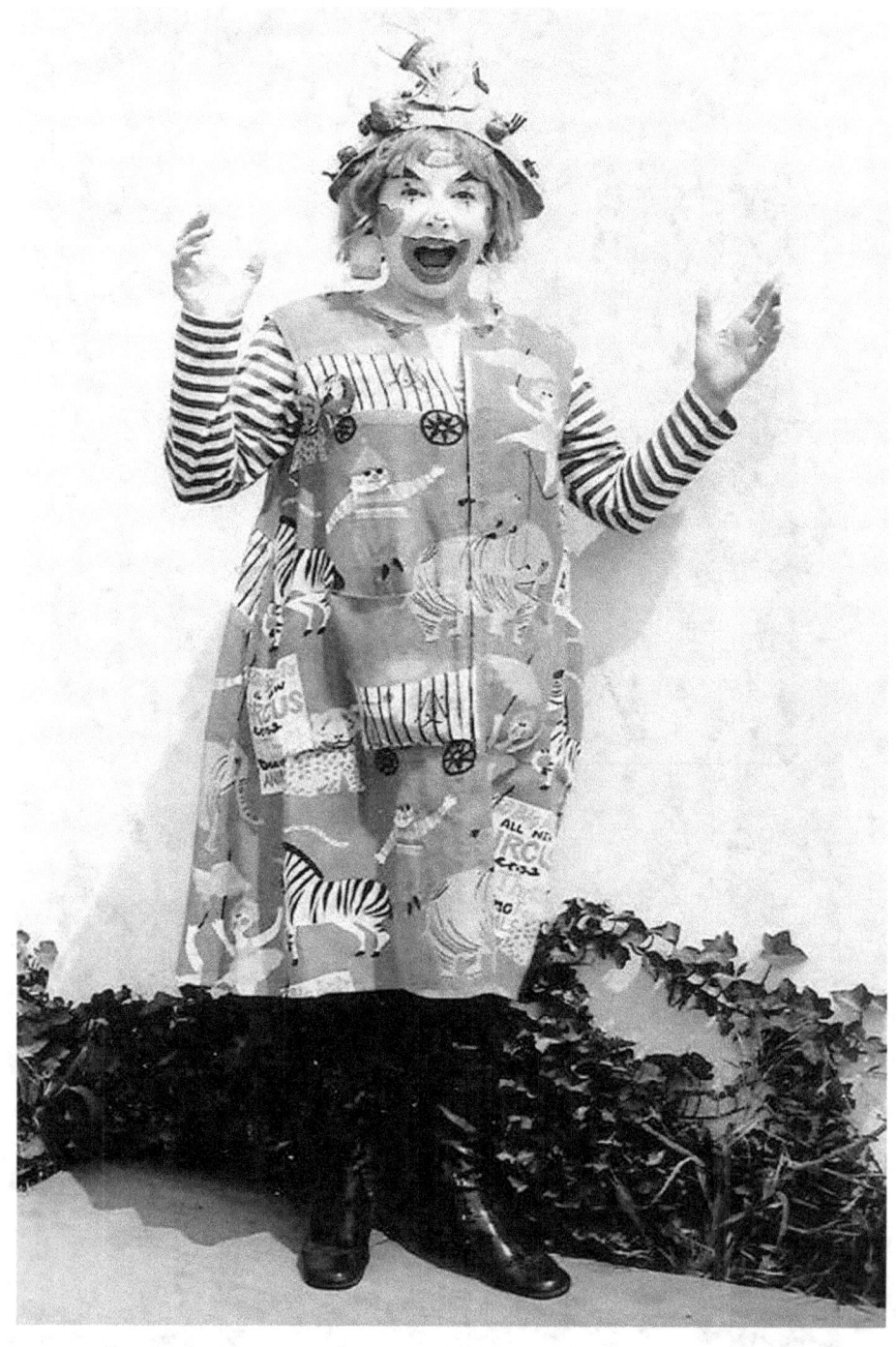

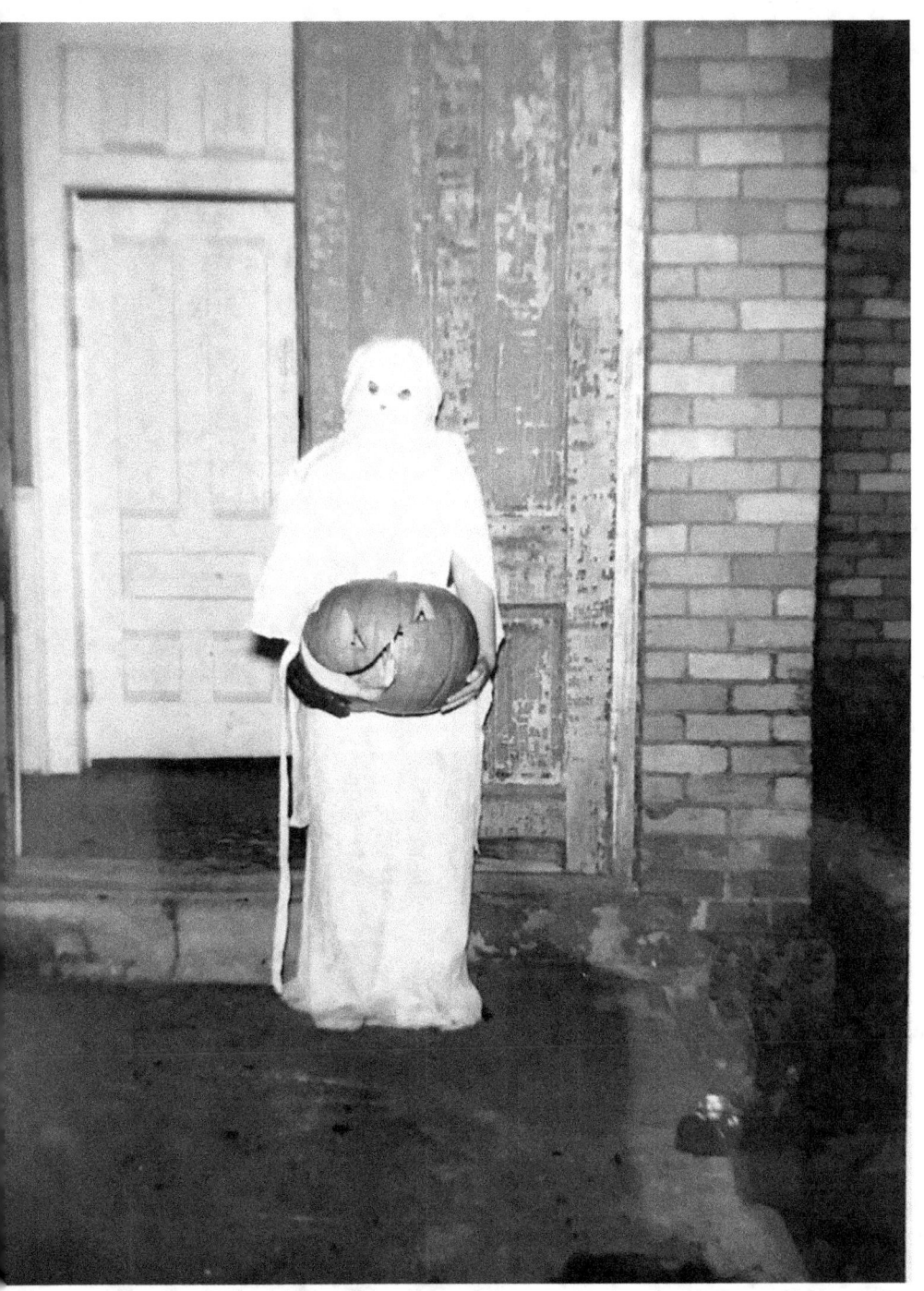

1966

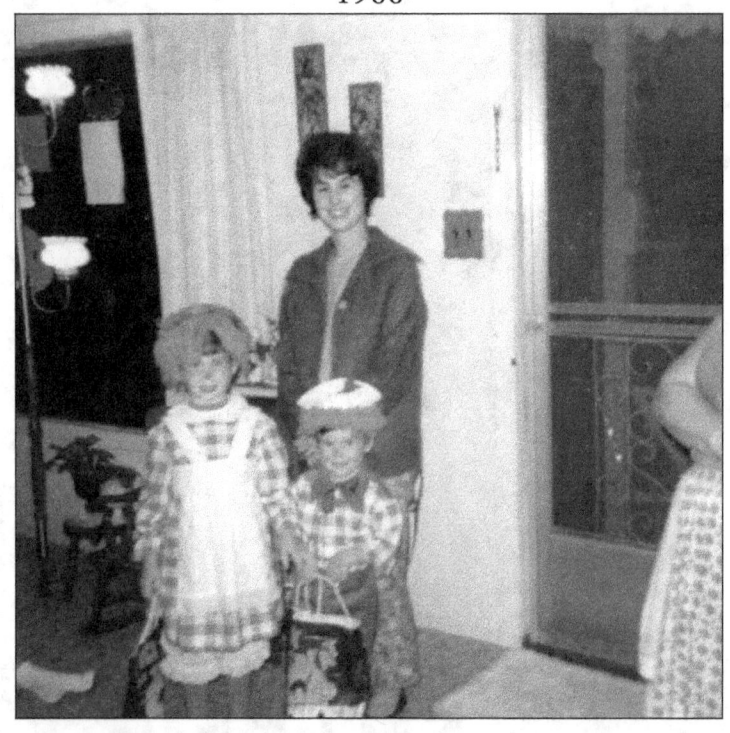

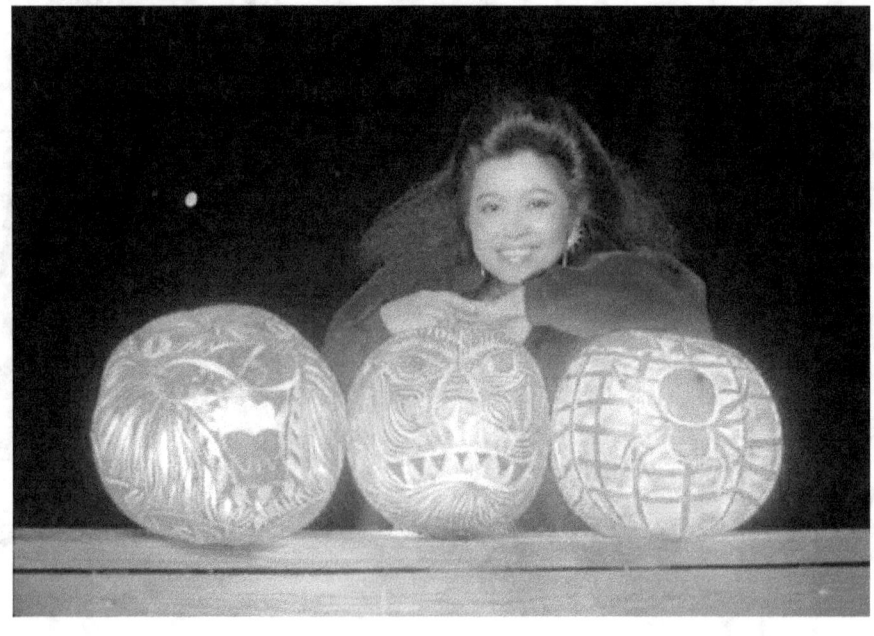

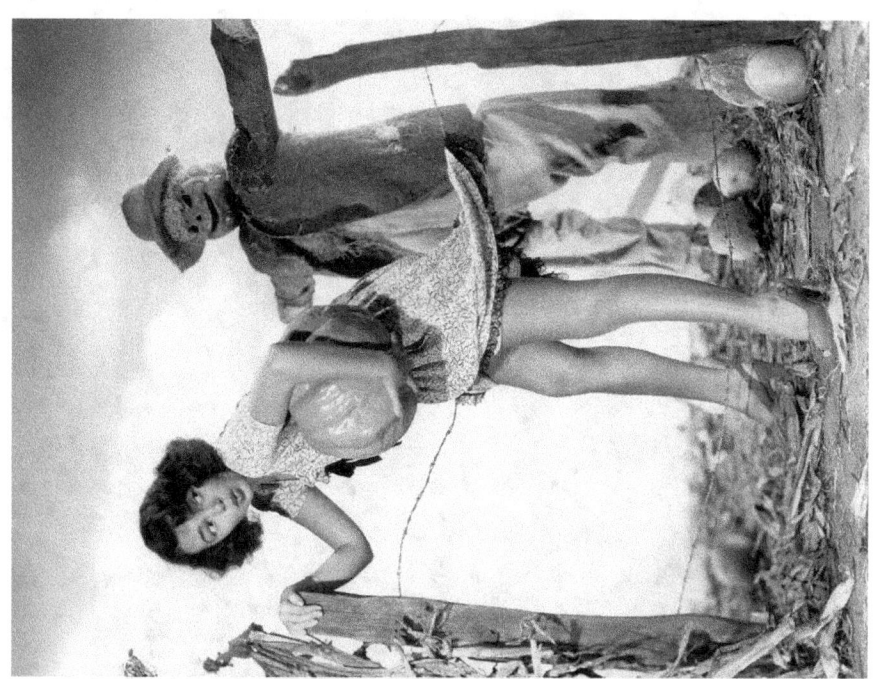

ABOVE: ACTRESS GLORIA SAUNDERS

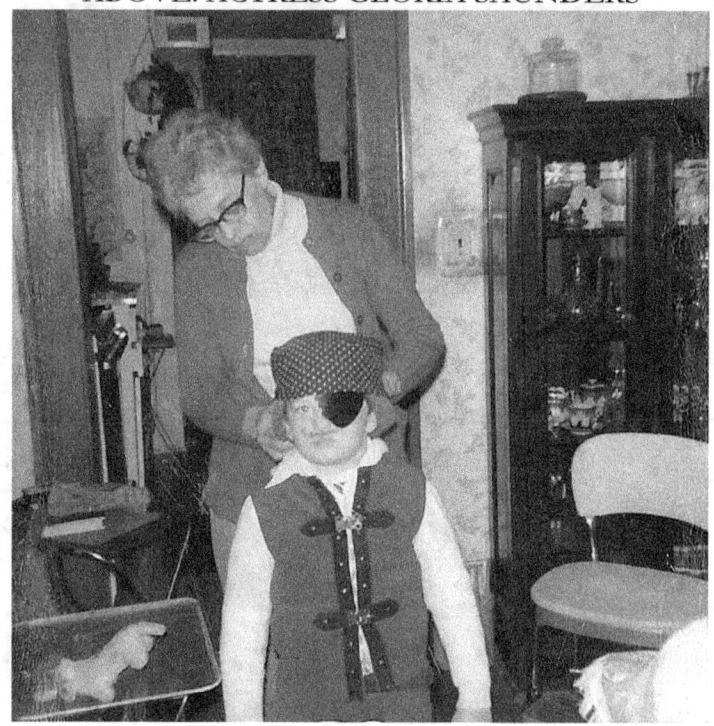

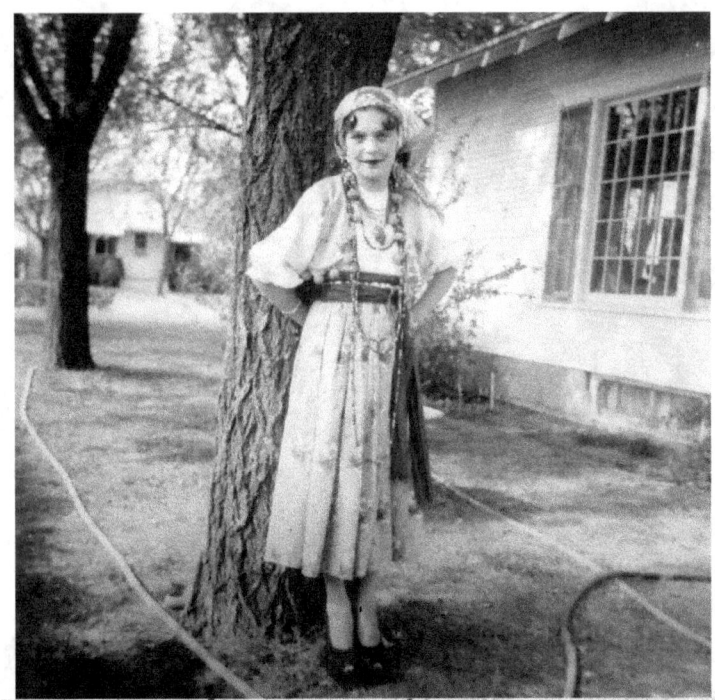

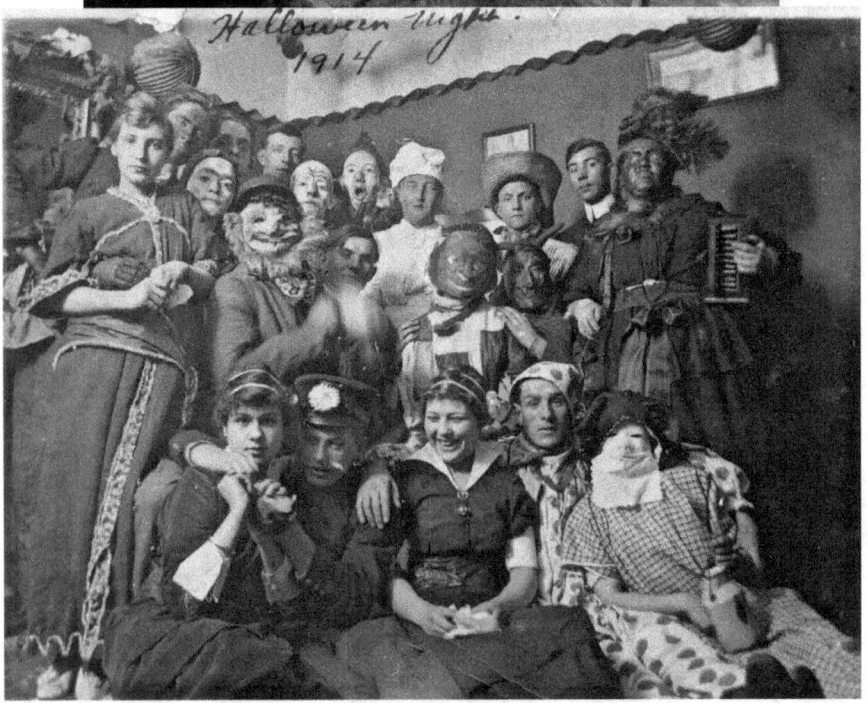

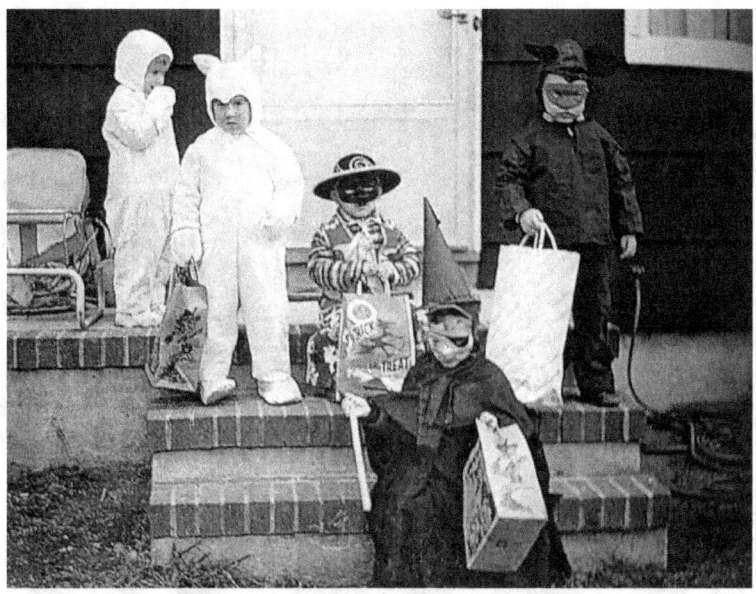

ABOVE: 1957 / BELOW: 1965

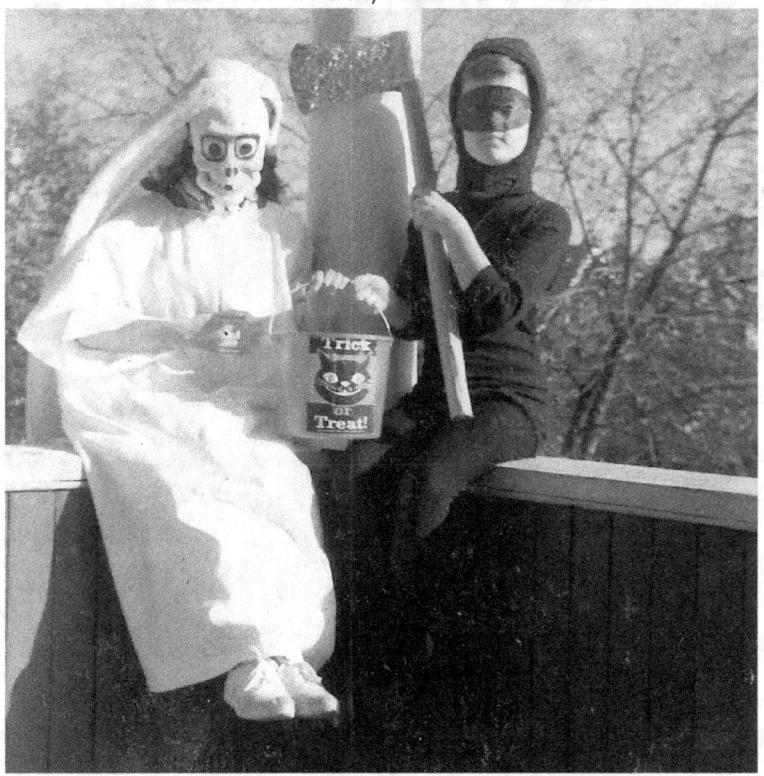

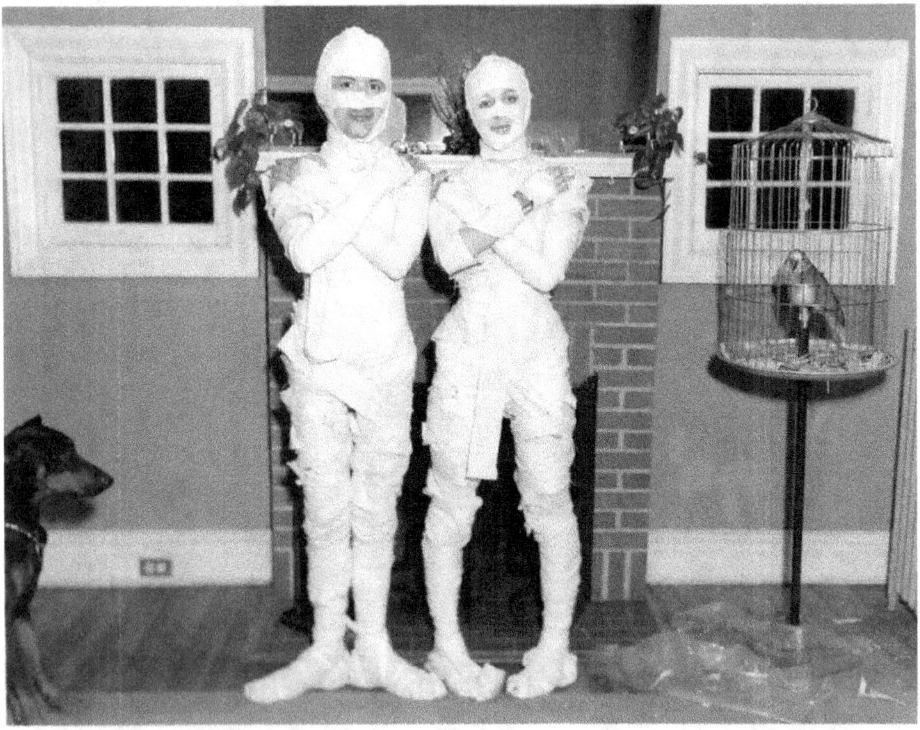

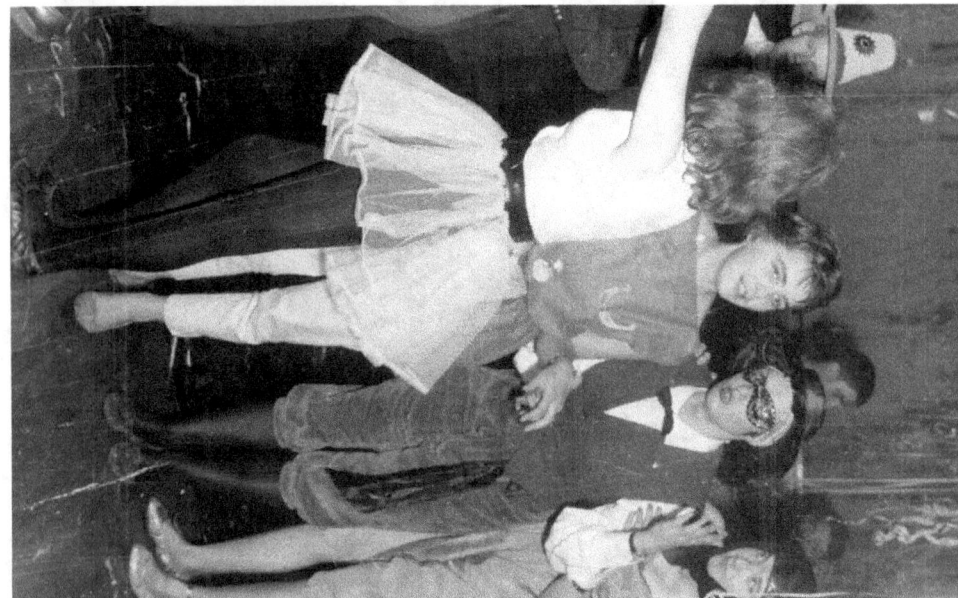

Vintage Halloween Photos

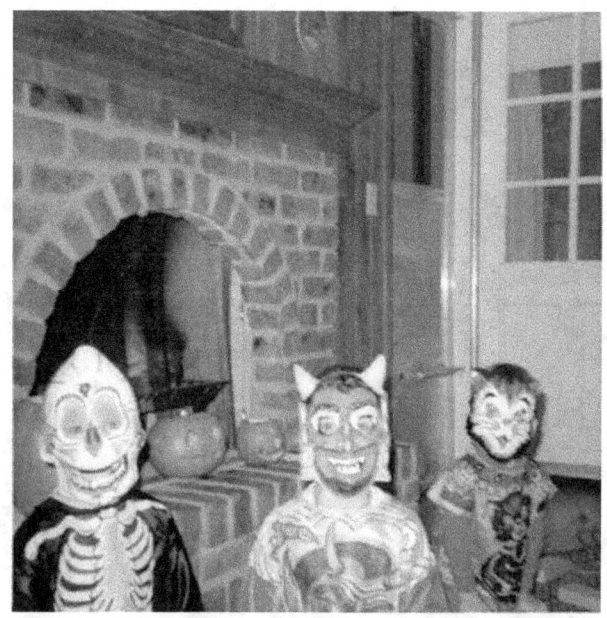

1969

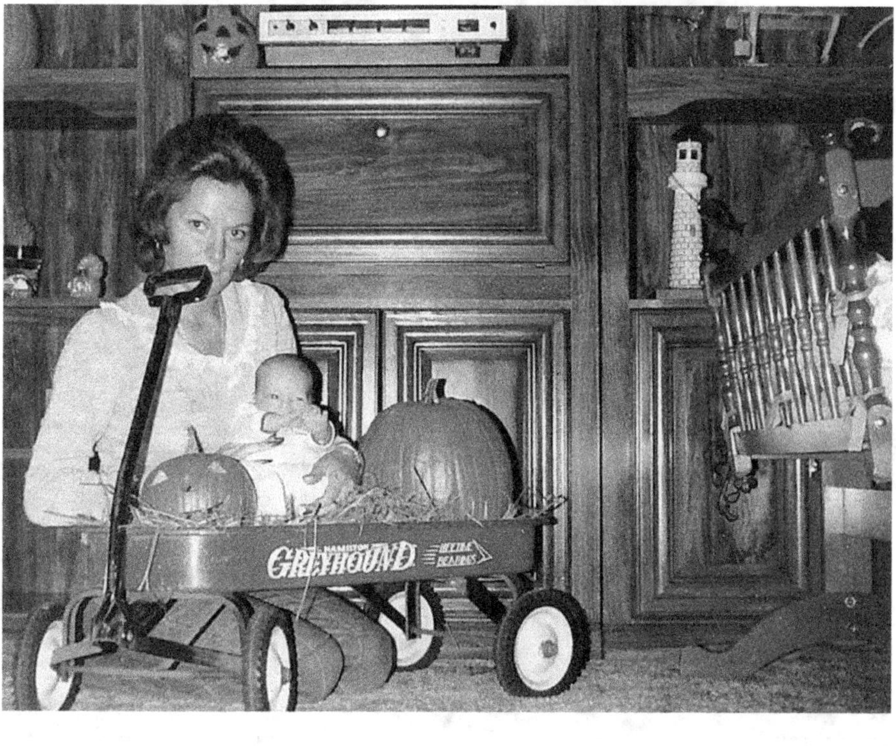

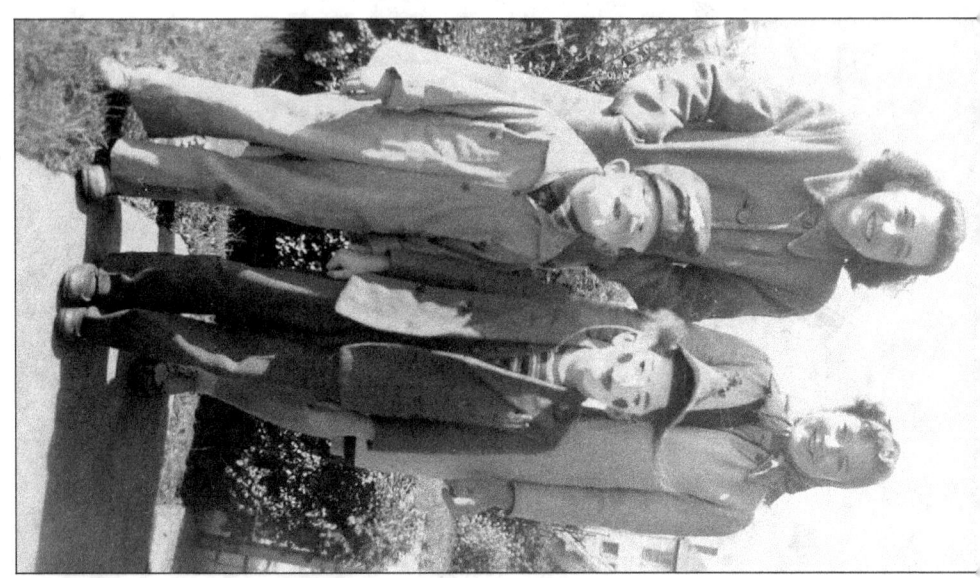

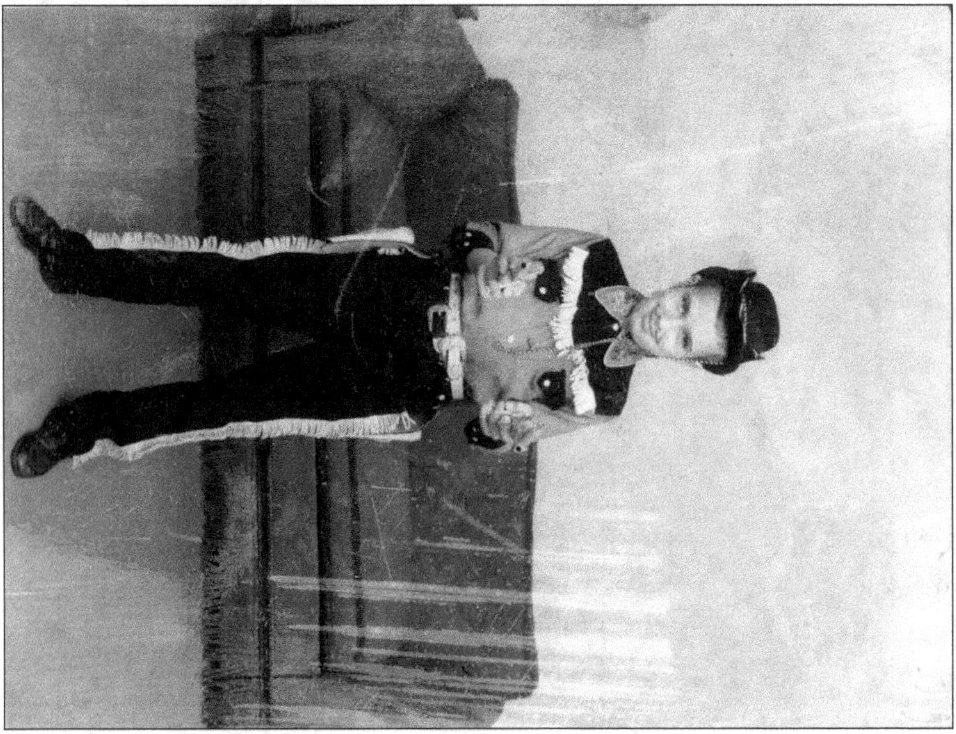

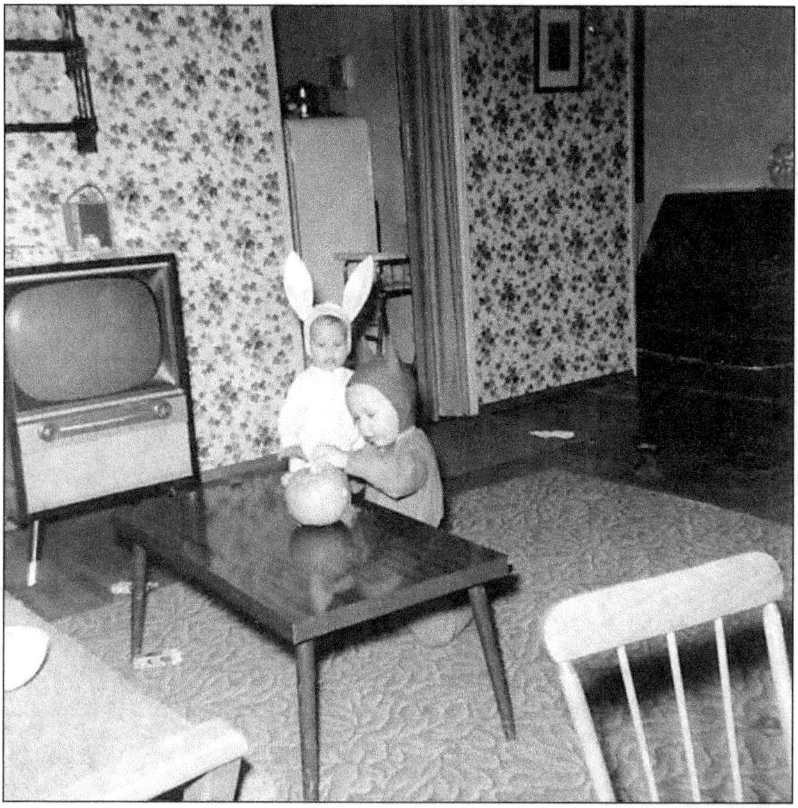

Vintage Halloween Photos

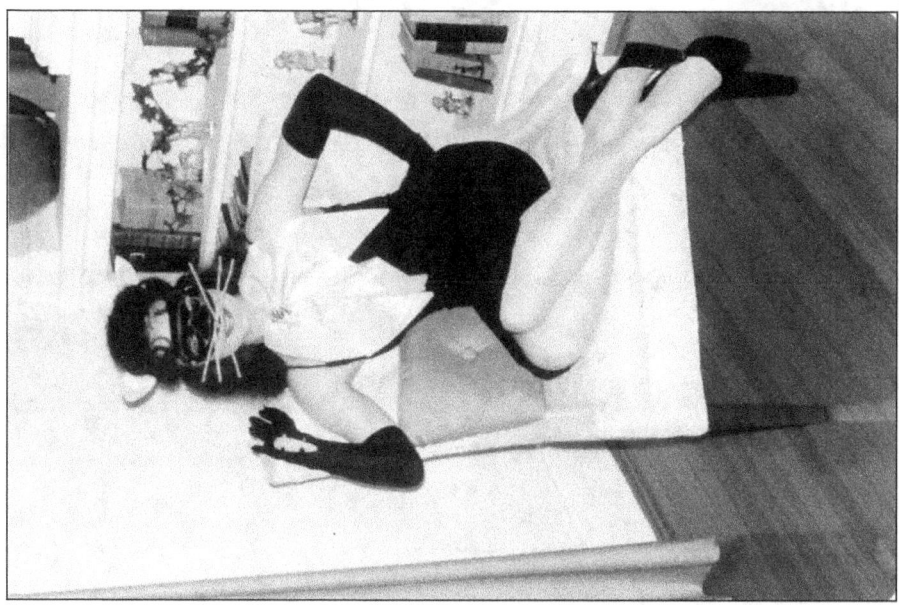

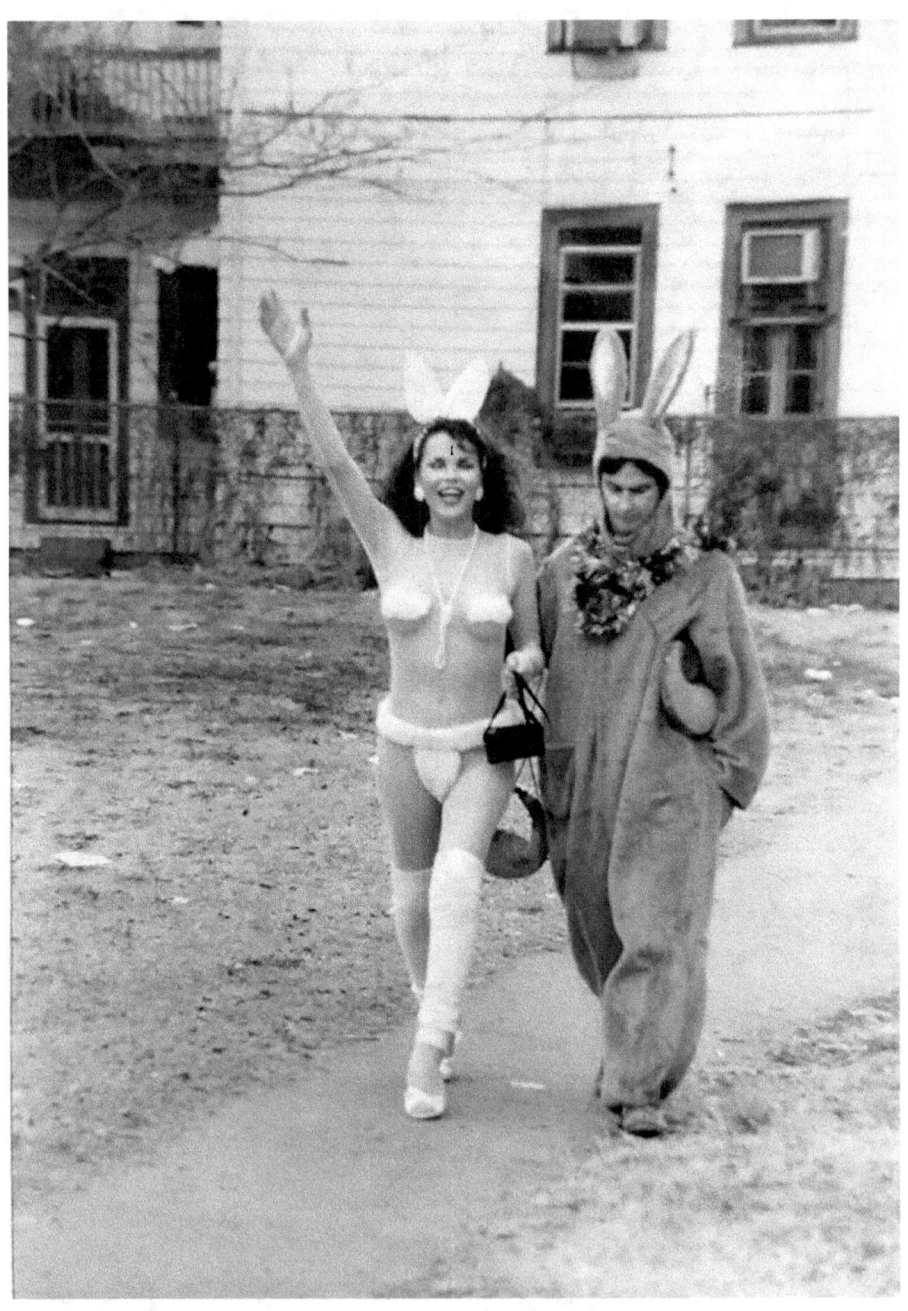

Vintage Halloween Photos

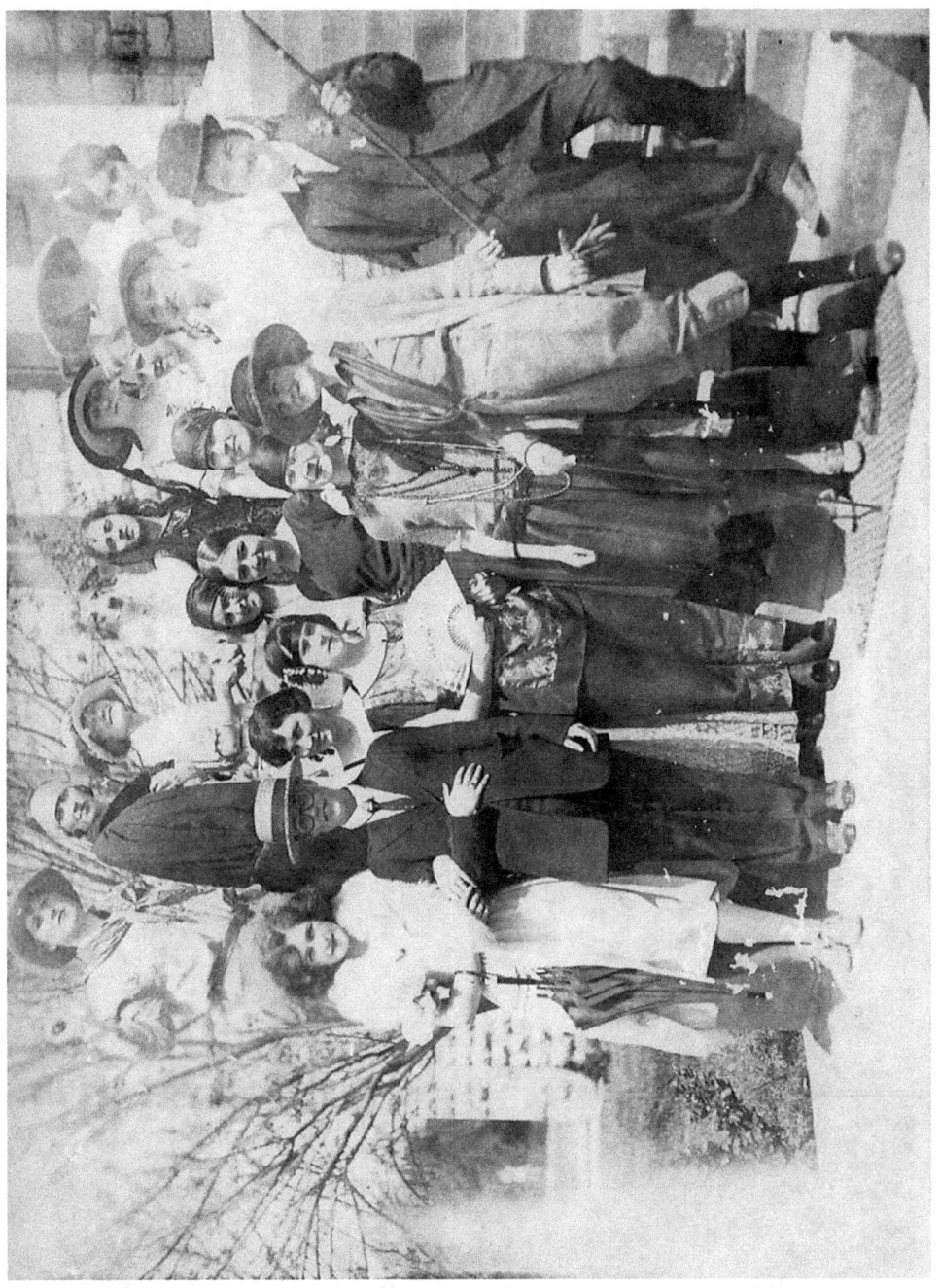

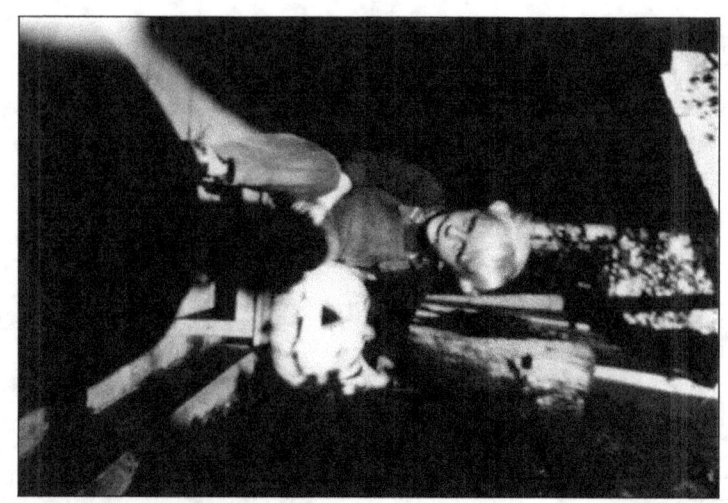

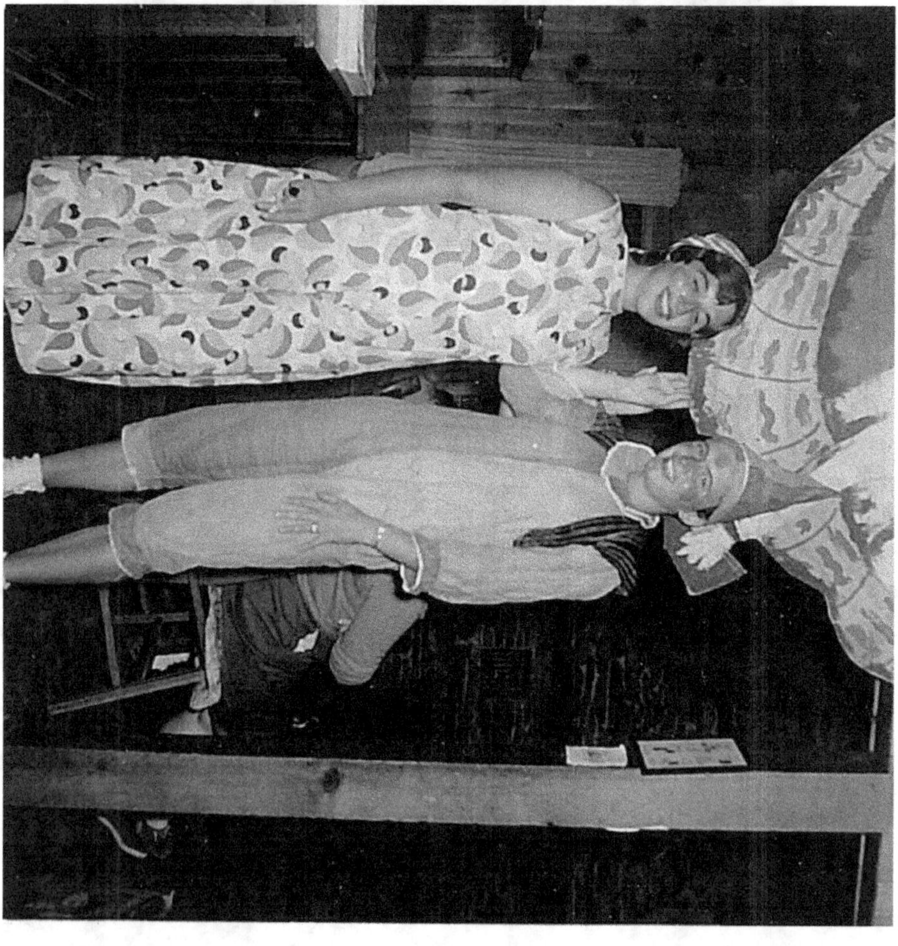

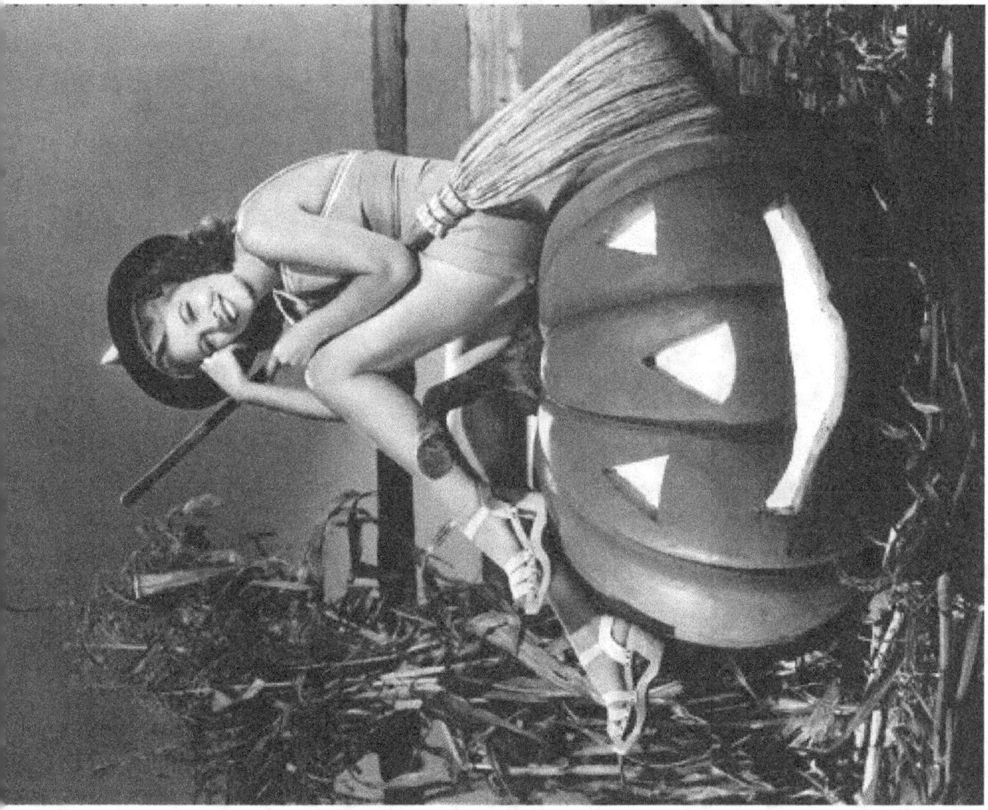

Vintage Halloween Photos

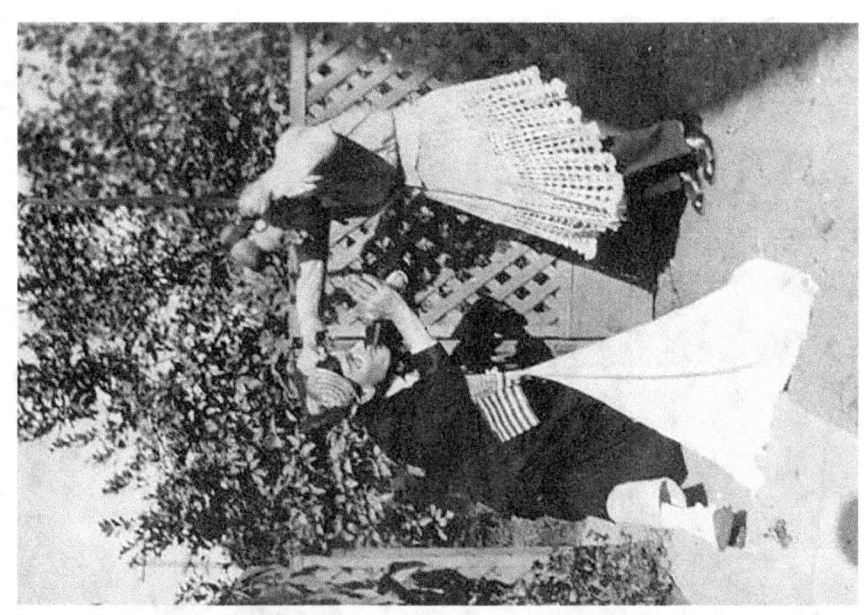

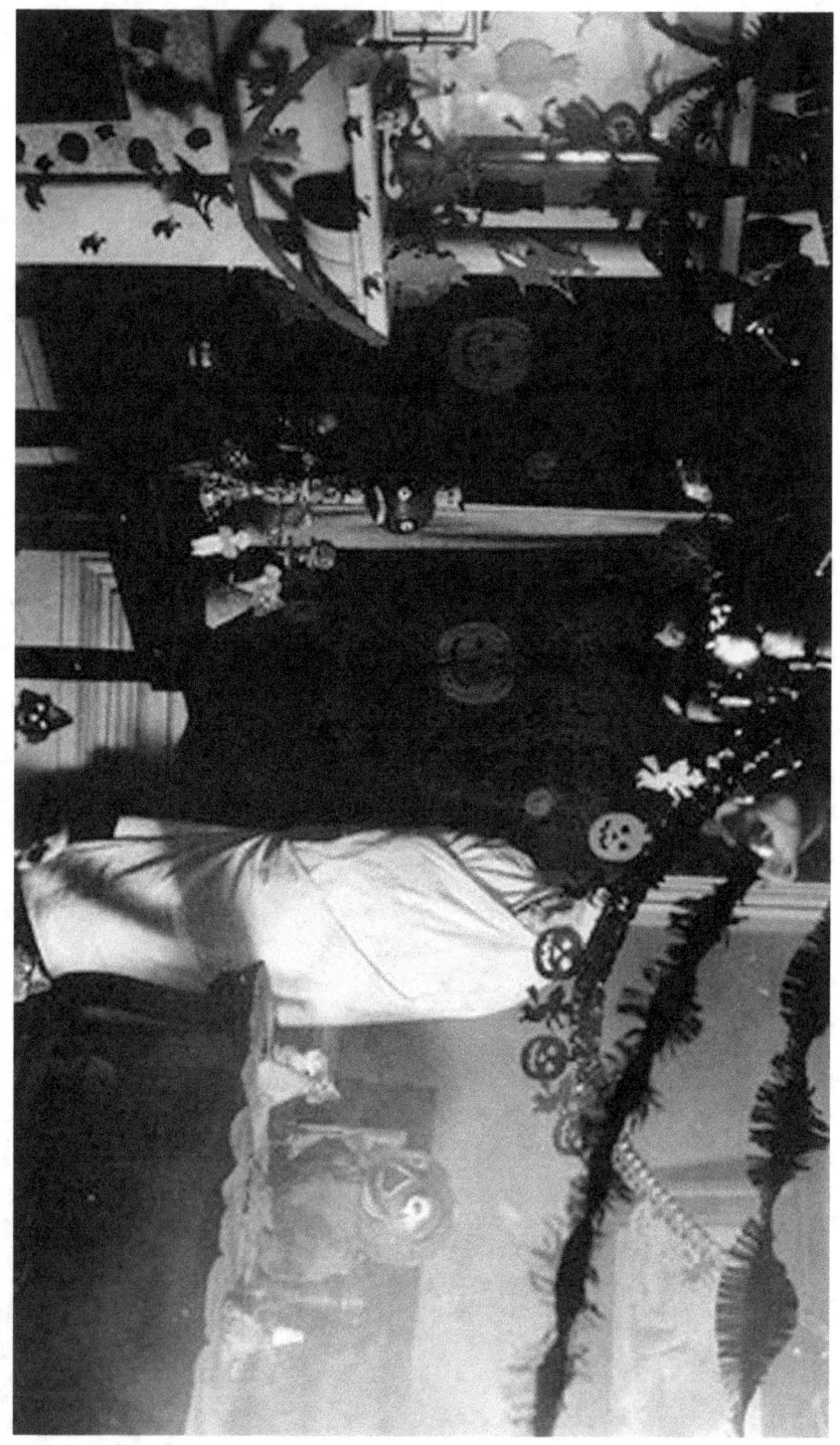

Vintage Halloween Photos

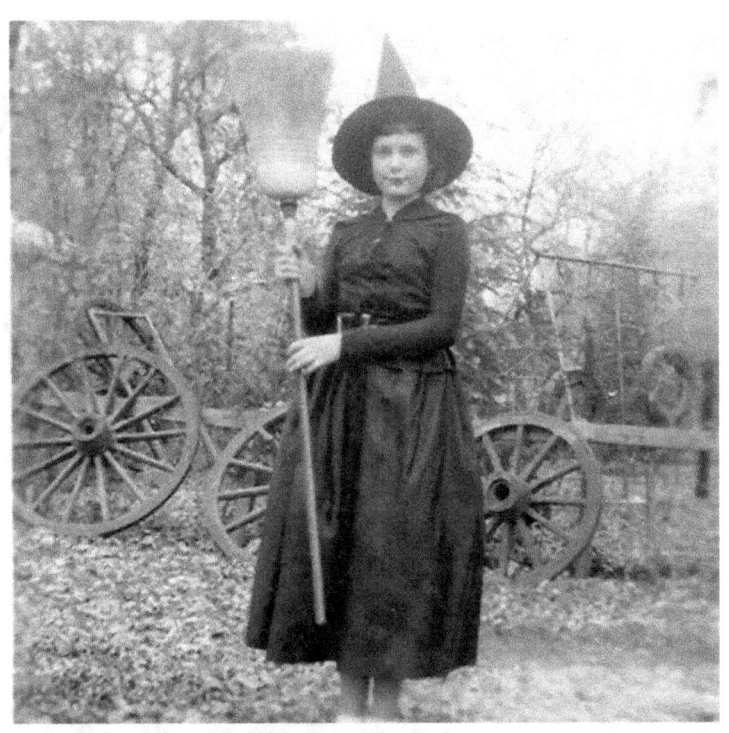

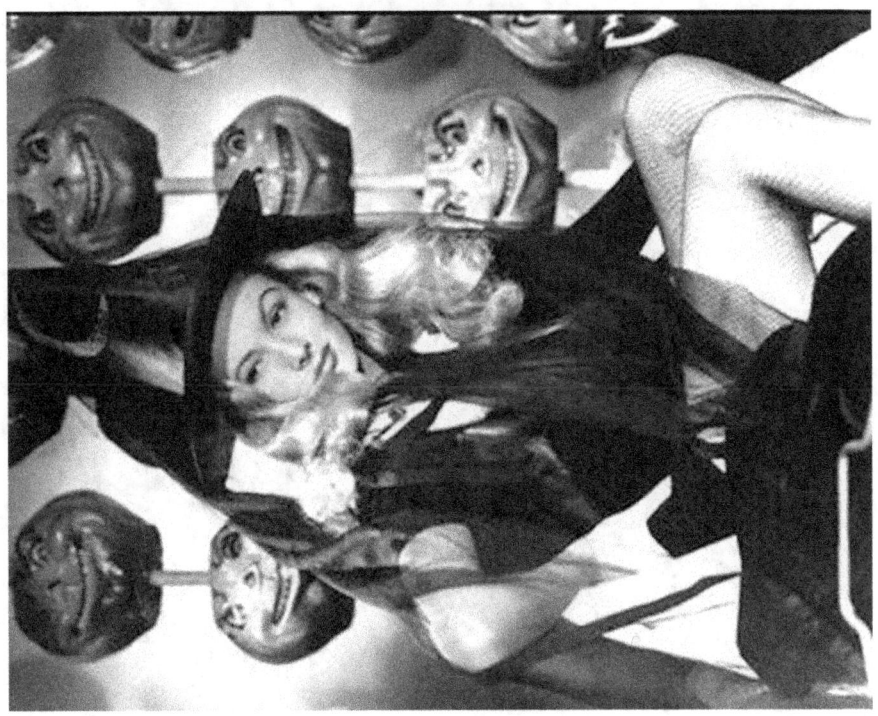

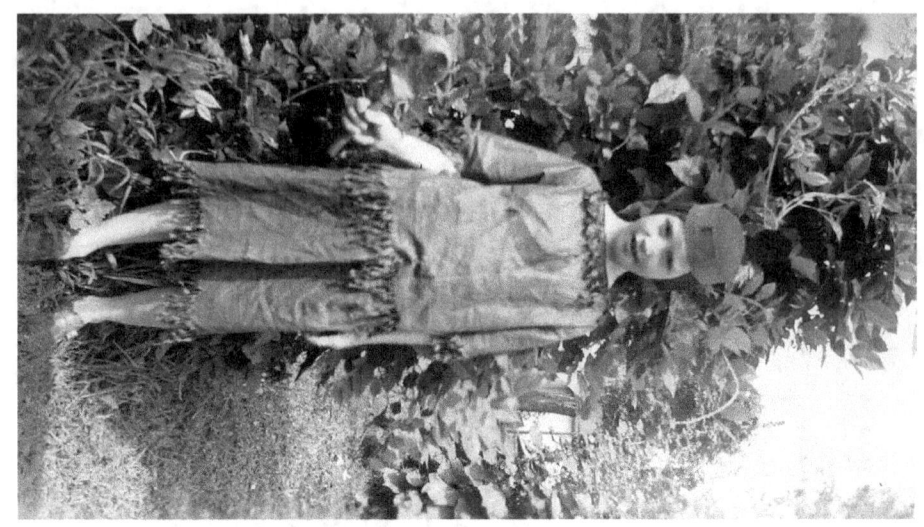

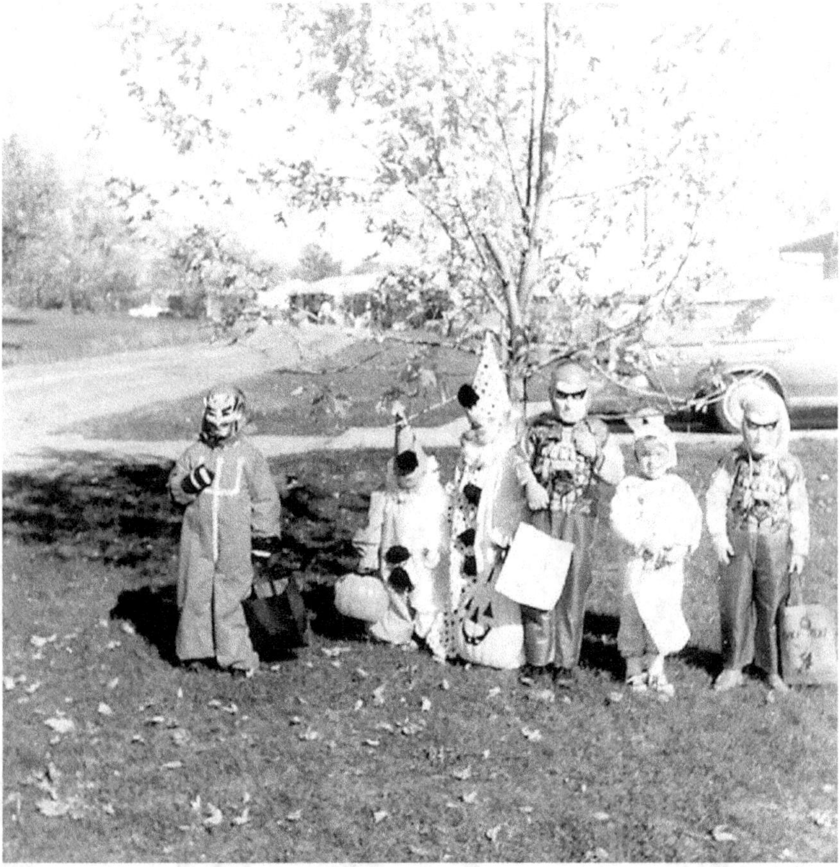

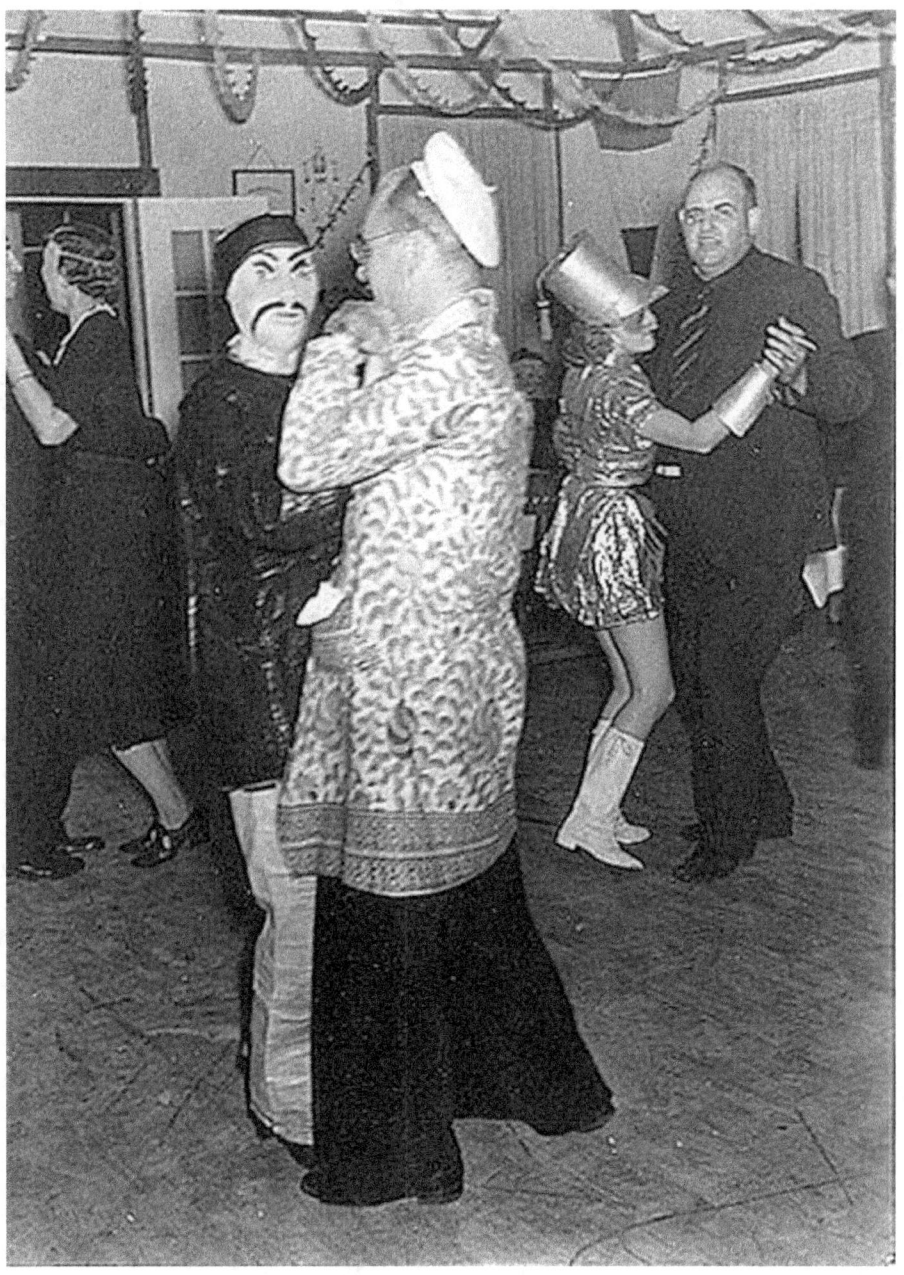

WYATT DOUGLAS

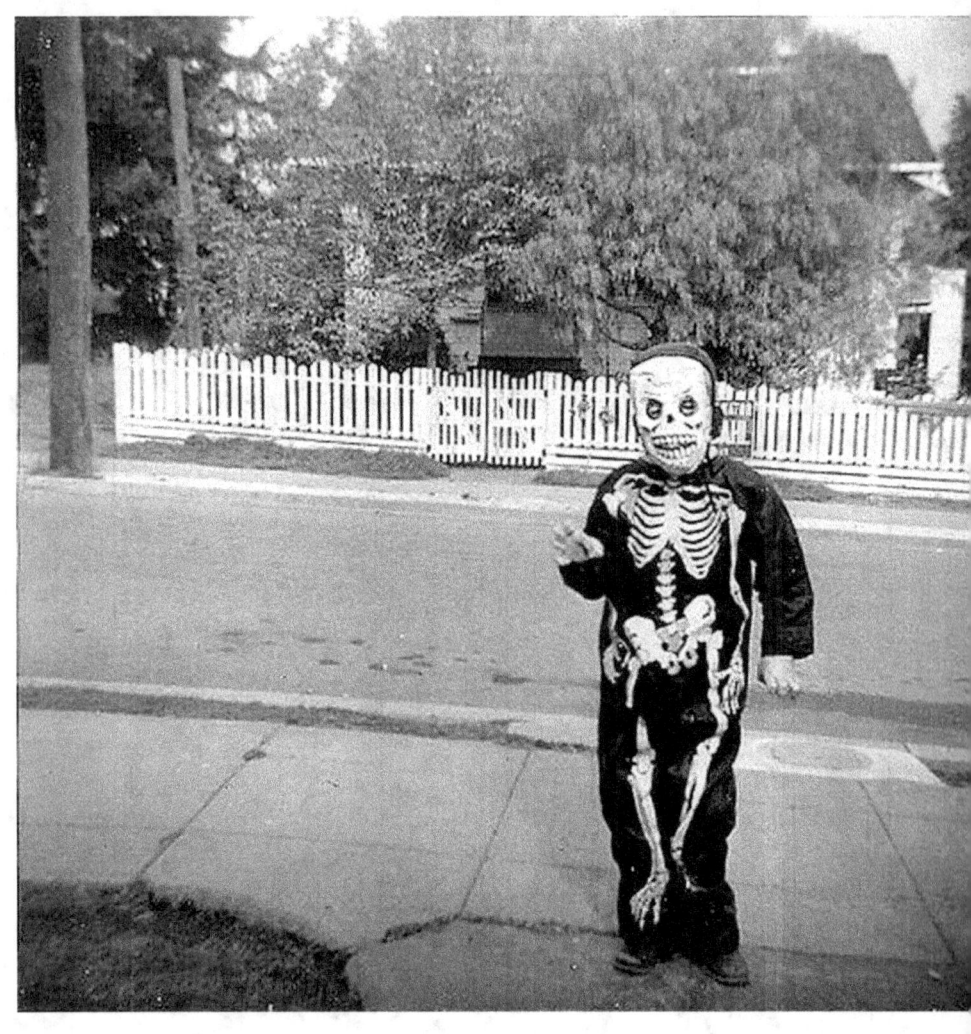

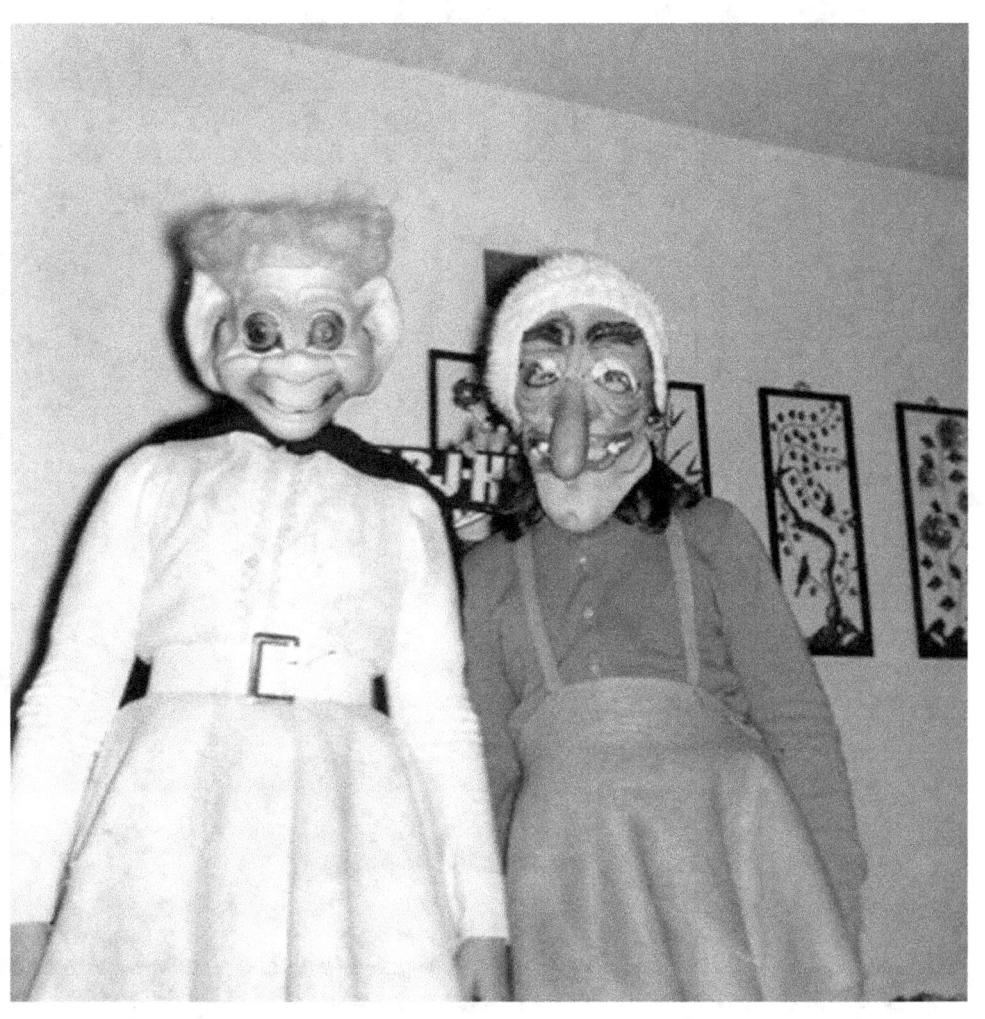

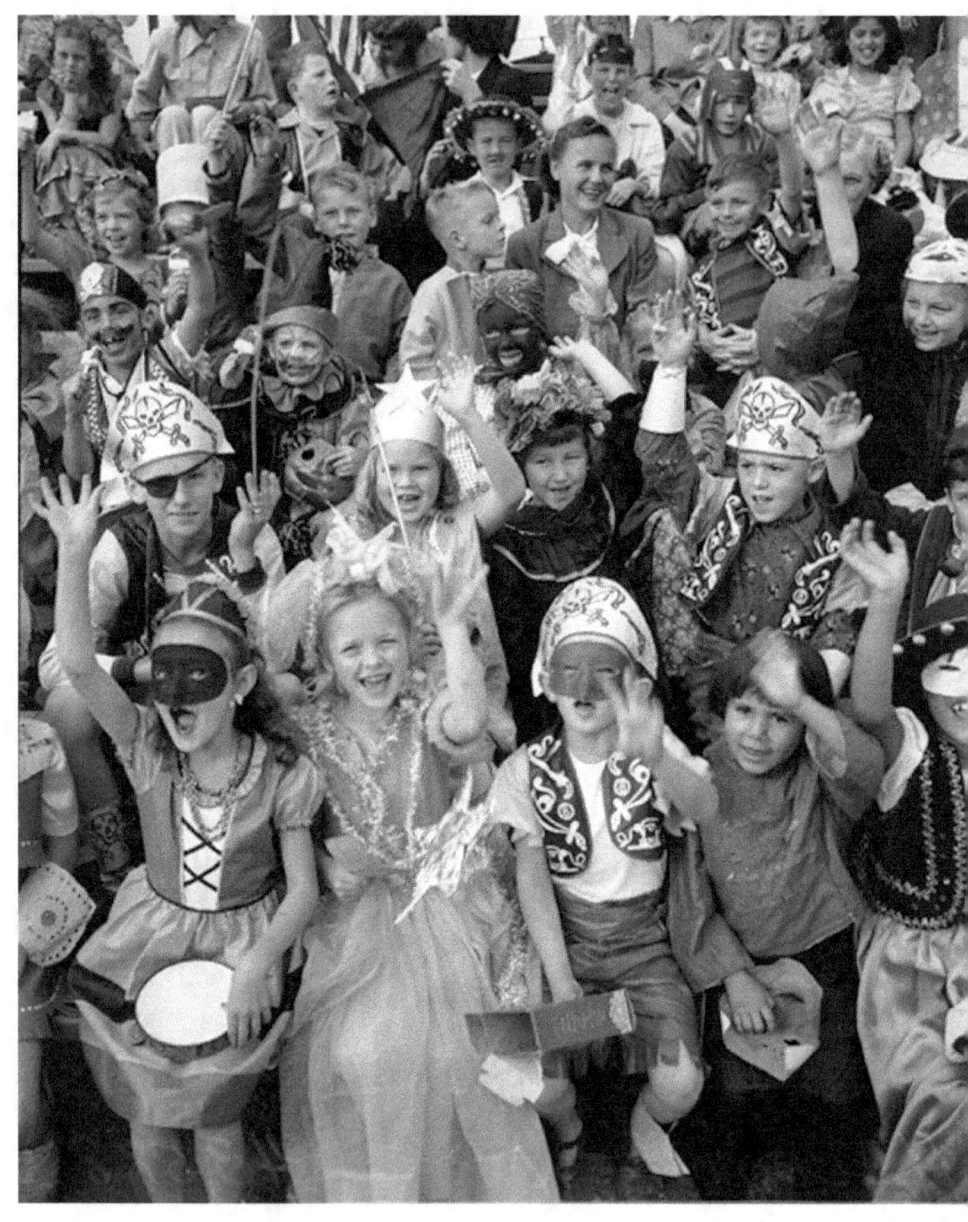

Vintage Halloween Photos

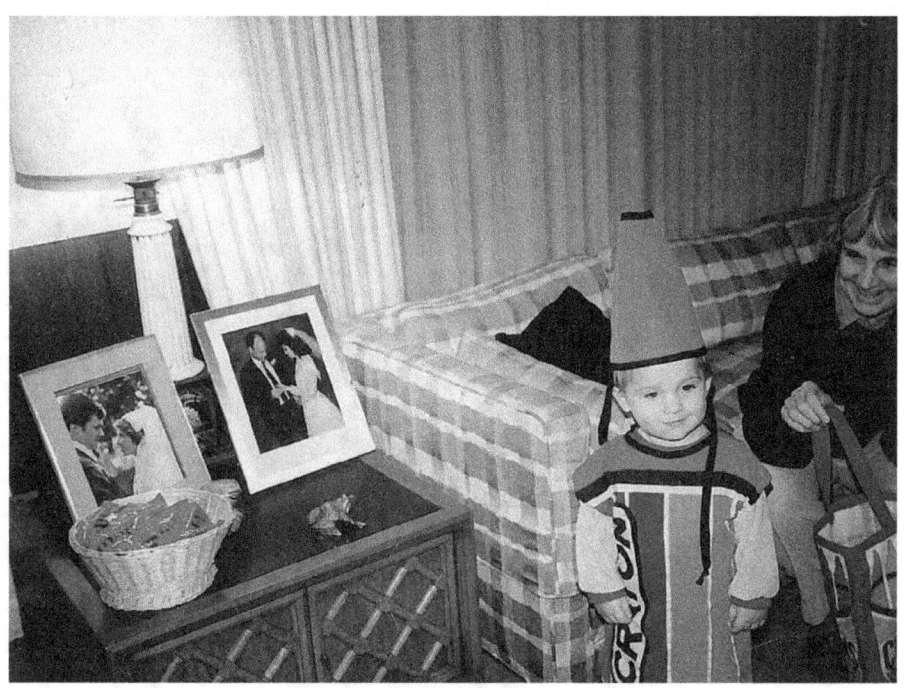

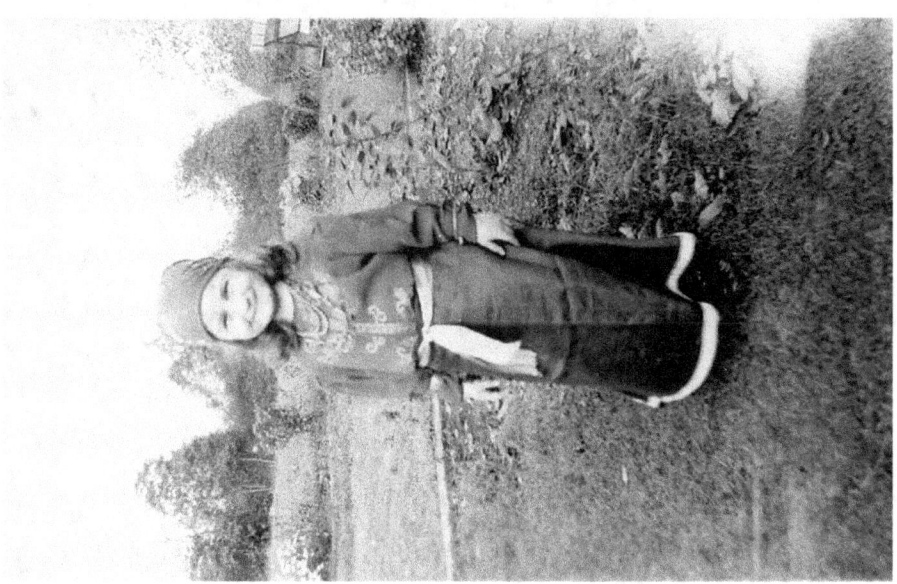

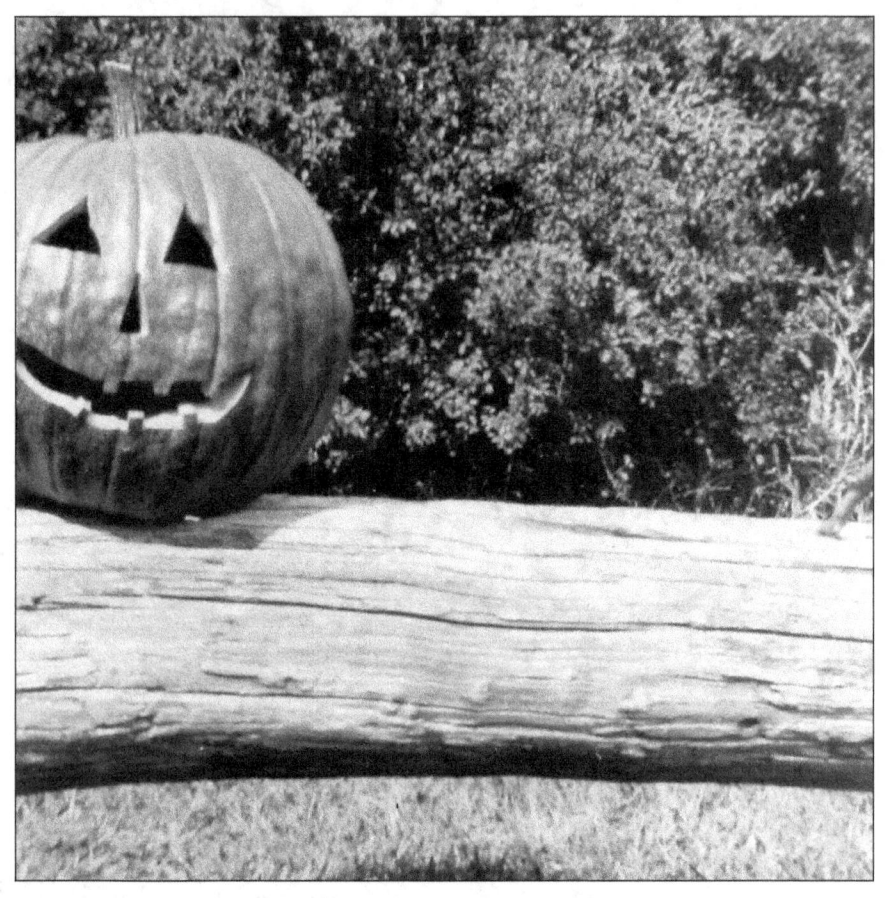

ABOUT THE AUTHOR

Wyatt Douglas is a researcher, archivist and historian.
He lives in Sunnyside Washington with his wife and two sons.

www.ingramcontent.com/pod-product-compliance
Lightning Source LLC
Chambersburg PA
CBHW071433220526
45469CB00004B/1517